Department of Education and Science
September 1978

Primary education in England

A survey by
HM Inspectors of Schools

London
Her Majesty's Stationery Office

ISBN 0 11 270484 0

Contents

Tables

Foreword

This report is an account of some aspects of the work of 7, 9 and 11 year old children in 1,127 classes in 542 schools so chosen as to be representative of primary schools in England. It gives information about the organisation of schools, the range of work done by the children, and the extent to which the work is matched to their abilities. It also includes an analysis of the scores obtained by children in objective tests administered by the National Foundation for Educational Research.

It is based on the direct observation of children's work by HM Inspectors experienced in primary education. The suggestions for the further development of that work reflect what was already successfully practised in a substantial number of classes and schools.

Inevitably some readers will be hoping to find information and judgements that do not appear; for example, although they will find comments about the help that parents gave in classes, they will not find discussion of the wider links between home and school, important though these are HM Inspectorate's major concern is the work done in institutions and classrooms. Furthermore, within the potential range of the work to be observed, HM Inspectors had to make decisions about priorities within the survey, taking into account the limitations of its manpower, and such circumstances as, in the case of French, the existence of a recent substantial report on the subject. Some parts of the curriculum are therefore treated more lightly than others, and accounts of the work of children in nursery classes, or in their first year of compulsory schooling, or in middle schools are not included.

What emerges from the report is that teachers in primary schools work hard to make pupils well behaved, literate and numerate. They are concerned for individual children, and especially for those who find it difficult to learn. If the schools are considered as a whole, it is clear that children are introduced to a wide range of knowledge and skills.

The efforts of children and teachers have produced encouraging results in the reading test for 11 year olds, where objective comparisons can be made with the past; there is no comparable objective evidence of past standards in other parts of the curriculum. In some aspects of the work the results overall are sometimes disappointing. The reasons for this vary, and rarely stem from inattention or poor effort. In some cases, the evidence clearly suggests that difficulty arises because individual teachers are trying to cover too much unaided. Some fairly modest re-adjustment of teachers' roles would allow those with special interests and gifts to use them more widely, as is shown in some classes where particularly success-ful work is done.

The report gives a national picture, but is addressed to those who carry responsibility at any level for decisions about education. In particular, it is hoped that teachers and heads of primary schools will, together with their local authority and its advisory and specialist services, consider how their work might be best developed in the light of the findings.

*　*　*　*

This report could not have been written without the cooperation of the many heads and teachers involved. We wish also to thank the NFER and a number of others whom we consulted, particularly Dr D Holt on the general statistical approach used, and Professor J Wrigley and Mr G F Peaker CBE, formerly HMI, on the results of the objective tests.

The authors alone are responsible for what has been made of the help received.

As with other reports published by HMI, no assumption can be made about government commitment to the provision of additional resources as a result of the survey.

1 The national survey

1.1 The main survey began in the autumn term of 1975, following pre-liminary feasibility and pilot studies, and was completed in the spring term of 1977.[1]

1.2 A three-stage random national sample was employed for the survey.[2] At the first stage a random, stratified sample of 542 schools was selected. Schools were classified by region and by the size of the year groups and included separate infant schools, combined junior with infant schools separate junior schools, first schools and combined first with middle schools. No separate middle schools were included.

1.3 The second stage involved selecting from within each school, subject to the age range, one class containing 7 year old children, one containing 9 year olds and one containing 11 year olds. This represented the end of the infant and junior stages of education and the intermediate stage at 9 years old. Where there were two or more classes in a school containing children of any of these ages, the class to be inspected was chosen randomly.[3] If children of more than one age group were contained in one class, only the work of the children of the age group relevant to this survey was inspected.

1.4 At the third stage sub-samples of 9 and 11 year old children were selected from among the children in the classes which had been inspected. The National Foundation for Educational Research administered objective tests of performance in reading at 9 and 11 years and mathematics at 11 years for these sub-samples [4]

---

[1] Appendix A, Feasibility and pilot surveys.
[2] Appendix B, The sample design.
[3] Appendix C, Administration.
[4] Appendix D, Weighting and calculation of standard errors.

1.5 The findings of the main report are based on information from 540 of the 542 schools in the sample and from 1,121 of the 1,127 classes which were inspected.[1] Since the three-stage sample was statistically representative, the findings reflect the situation in English primary schools at the time of the survey.[2]

1.6 Individual pupils, schools or local education authorities are not identified in the report. In the early stages of the exercise there was consultation with associations representing teachers, educational advisory services and local authorities and, during the course of the survey, with the schools and local education authorities actually involved.

1.7 The head of each school and the relevant class teachers completed questionnaires providing information about their professional experience, the school and the classes containing the teaching groups selected for the survey.[3] Each of these teaching groups was inspected by two of HM Majesty's Inspectors who made an agreed return using schedules designed for the survey. These schedules were constructed by HM Inspectors on the basis of their knowledge of primary schools and teaching and on their collective experience of assessing the work of children in primary schools. The items in them are concerned with the curriculum, teaching methods and school organisation. The schedules are described in detail in Annex B.[4]

1.8 The length of time which HM Inspectors spent in a school depended on the age-range and size of the school and varied from one and a half to three days. In order that the full range of work being done could be inspected and recorded, the schedules were more comprehensive in what they contained than any individual class was likely to be in a position to provide; moreover some classes had to be visited during the autumn term when only a small part of their programme for the year had been completed. It also has to be recognised that some types of work are more readily available for inspection than others: children's written work can be examined in their books, some paintings and models are likely to be displayed; but other kinds of work, particularly in spoken language, music and physical education, usually have to be observed in progress in order for any evaluation of quality to take place. HM Inspectors assessed the quality of work only when they were able to inspect this for themselves.[5]

[1] Appendix E, Withdrawal and replacement of schools, and response rate.
[2] Appendix F, Comparison of the survey sample and National estimates.
[3] Appendix C and Annex A.
[4] See also Chapter 6i and Appendix C.
[5] Appendix C and Annex B.

1.9 The information obtained from heads, class teachers, HM Inspectors and from the objective tests administered by NFER was processed by computer and appropriate statistical techniques were employed.[1]

---

[1] Appendix G, Methods of analysis.

2 The schools and the teachers

i THE SCHOOLS

2.1 Schools provide the environment in which children work and learn. The characteristics of primary schools vary considerably from the small rural school with fewer than ten children to the exceptionally large school which may cater for over eight hundred pupils. Some children are accommodated in newly built schools, others in buildings put up a hundred years ago, some of which have been modernised and renovated, others not. In some schools children are taught in separate classrooms, in others children work in shared teaching spaces supplemented by withdrawal areas.

2.2 Primary schools have to provide for children with a wide variety of different needs, including those of the physically and mentally handicapped, some of whom may at some time require provision in a special unit or school, and those of the exceptionally able. The children also reflect the characteristics of different sorts of family background and of the neighbourhood from which they come.

2.3 The type of school in which children are taught also varies; some attend one combined infant and junior school up to the age of eleven years, while others transfer from a separate infant to a separate junior school at the age of seven. A minority of children attend a first school and may transfer to a middle school at the age of eight or nine; a few children attend a combined first and middle school up to the age of twelve or thirteen.

2.4 Of the schools in the survey sample, half were combined junior with infant schools, the majority of which were small schools with no more than one-form entry; in contrast most of the separate junior and separate infant schools were two-form entry or larger. Figure 1 in the Annex to this Chapter shows the proportion of the different types of school included in the survey.

Figure 1 Division of sample schools by type of organisation.

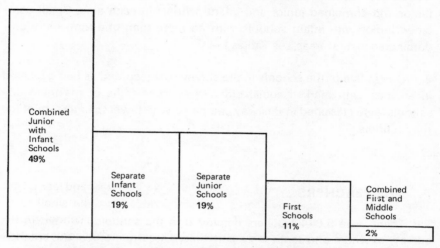

Note: The percentages have been rounded and do not necessarily total to a hundred.

2.5 During the survey the locality of each school was classified as inner city, 'other urban' or rural[1]. The distribution among the three kinds of locality is shown in Figure 2.

Figure 2 *Schools in the sample classified by locality*

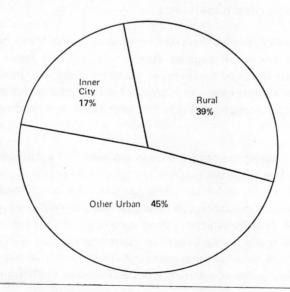

[1] See Appendix H, Definition of locality.

2.6 Within inner city and 'other urban' areas there was a similar pattern of distribution with substantial proportions of separate infant, separate junior and combined junior and infant schools in each area. Small combined junior with infant schools with no more than one form entry predominated in rural areas, see Tables 1 – 3.

2.7 One in five of the schools in the survey was recorded as being located in an area with marked social difficulties; three-fifths of the inner city schools were classified in this way compared with fewer than a tenth of the rural schools.

ii. THE TEACHERS

2.8 There were 5,844 teachers employed in the schools included in the survey, of whom one-tenth were part-time. Three-quarters of the teachers in the schools were women. The class teachers of the selected 7, 9 and 11 year old classes formed a quarter of all the teachers in the survey schools. Seven year old classes were taught almost exclusively by women teachers while 11 year old classes were taught by nearly equal numbers of men and women teachers, see Table 4.

Qualifications and experience

2.9 One-tenth of the teachers were graduates and, of these, two-fifths held Bachelor of Education degrees. Graduate status was more usual among more recently qualified teachers; of those teachers with more than fifteen years service slightly over one in twenty held a graduate qualification, while one in five of the teachers in their first year of teaching was a graduate, see Table 5.

2.10 Over three-quarters of the class teachers had originally been trained to teach the age range with which they were working, see Table 6. Allowing that some flexibility to transfer to an age group for which teachers were not initially trained is desirable, this reflects a reasonable degree of consistency between the work for which teachers were originally trained and that which they were actually doing. Where teachers were teaching in an age group other than that for which they were initially trained there was no evidence that this affected the standard of work achieved by the children.[1]

---

[1] See Annex to Chap. 7 Note 2.

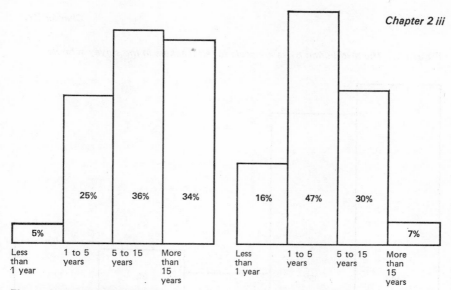

	25%	36%	34%		16%	47%	30%
5%							7%

| Less than 1 year | 1 to 5 years | 5 to 15 years | More than 15 years | Less than 1 year | 1 to 5 years | 5 to 15 years | More than 15 years |

Figure 3. *Length of total teaching experience of all teachers in the survey schools.* **Figure 4.** *Length of time spent in present school of all teachers in the survey schools.*

2.11 One teacher in twenty had taught for less than a year; nearly three-quarters of the teachers had more than five years teaching experience. Over a third of the teachers had taught in the same school for longer than five years and nearly half had taught in the schools in which they were then employed for between one and five years.

2.12 There was evidence during the period of the survey that the proportion of teachers who were newly appointed to the schools was decreasing, resulting in greater staffing stability within particular schools.[1]

Allocation of posts

2.13 At the time of the Survey, teachers were paid on a series of salary scales rising from Scale 1 to Scale 4, and beyond that to Deputy Head and Head. The number of teachers paid on Scale 2 and above in a particular school depended, in accordance with the Burnham Report, on the number of pupils on roll in recent years. Teachers in primary schools with 350 or fewer pupils were normally restricted to Scale 1 and Scale 2. Teachers above Scale 1 usually, though not necessarily, carried responsibilities for additional duties. Figure 5 shows the distribution by salary scale of all teachers in the Survey schools. The distribution between men and women teachers is shown in Table 7.

---

[1]See Annex to Chapter 7, Note 5.

Figure 5. *The distribution by salary scale for all teachers in the survey schools.*

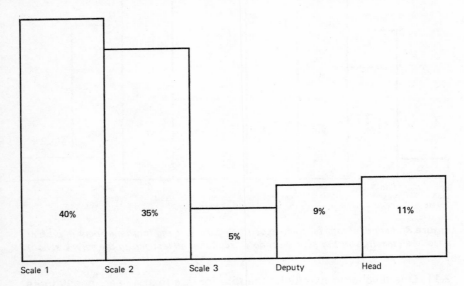

Scale 1   Scale 2   Scale 3   Deputy   Head

40%   35%   5%   9%   11%

Note : Scale 4 posts less than 0.5%

2.14 Teachers undertook a range of responsibilities, in addition to those for their own class or their particular teaching duties, in connection with organisational matters affecting the whole or a major part of the school or in connection with the curriculum. The distribution of posts carrying special responsibilities for areas of the curriculum is discussed in Chapter 4 i. The influence of teachers with special responsibilities is examined in Chapter 7 vi and Chapter 8 viii paragraphs 45-47.

2.15 The size and type of school influenced the kind of organisational posts allocated within individual schools. Teachers with special responsibility for an infant or junior department were normally found within a combined junior with infant school, while responsibility for year groups occurred mainly in three-form entry or larger schools. Posts of responsibility for an infant department were found predominantly in two-form entry or smaller schools.

2.16 Just over a half of the schools had teachers carrying responsibility for oversight of the library and just over a quarter for books and materials within a resource area intended to service the needs of a group of classes or the whole school. Both types of responsibility were more common in larger schools. There were very few teachers with responsibility for the organisation of arrangements to meet the needs of the very able pupils : these pupils were usually catered for within the normal classroom. [1] There were more instances where special arrangements for the less able pupils were employed. These included the withdrawal of groups and individuals for special tuition. Two-fifths of the schools had teachers with responsibility for the organisation of the remedial work within a school. About a half of two-form entry and smaller schools had a member of staff with overall responsibility for the infant classes, see Table 8.

iii. ACCOMMODATION AND RESOURCES

2.17 About four out of five of the classes selected for the survey were in accommodation which was considered reasonably adequate for the normal work undertaken by the class; in two-fifths of these classes the accommodation positively facilitated the work of the teachers and children. Nine out of ten of the classes worked in separate classrooms, the remainder being accommodated in open or semi-open working spaces shared by two or more classes. Slightly more than a tenth of the classes were situated in classrooms which were on a separate site from the main school building and a similar proportion were housed in hutted accommodation. In the classrooms that were found not to be reasonably adequate, the space was such that it imposed limitations on what could be undertaken.[2]

2.18 In few schools, less than one in five, had adaptation been made for educational use, other than for physical education, of the space surrounding the school, whether playgrounds, grassed areas or playing fields.

2.19 The available material resources – general equipment and apparatus, audio-visual and other teaching materials – were considered to be adequate for four out of five classes. In just under one in ten of these the material resources in the school were particularly good and facilitated a variety of work undertaken by the children. When the inner city, 'other urban' and rural schools were considered separately it was found that a higher proportion of inner city schools was generally less satisfactory than in other areas; but a larger proportion of inner city schools than schools in other areas was in the category with particularly good resources. This probably

---

[1] See Annex to Chapter 3 Table 17.
[2] The results of a more detailed study of the stock of school buildings, based on a ten per cent sample of all schools, were published in 'A Study of School Building' (HMSO 1977).

reflects the policy of allocating additional resources to designated schools in social priority areas and the resulting improvement in the standard of provision in these particular schools.

2.20 In over half the schools reasonable care was taken to arrange materials and displays of work to provide an interesting and lively learning environment for the children. Some schools made considerable efforts to enhance their surroundings in this way, sometimes in unpromising circumstances. Vandalism outside school hours was a limiting factor in the creation of an attractive and effective learning environment in one school in ten of the total samlpe; vandalism was one and a half times as common in schools located in inner city areas as in those situated in 'other urban' areas and five times as common in inner city schools as in schools located in rural areas.

iv. SPECIAL ENGLISH LANGUAGE NEEDS

2.21 An important educational consideration for some schools was the facility with which children of families of overseas origin spoke and used the English language. A third of all the schools in the survey had some children on roll for whom English was not their first language. A very small minority of schools had a substantial proportion of such pupils. Just under a fifth of the schools contained children whose first language was a European language other than English; this is a similar proportion to those having children whose first language originated in the Indian sub-continent. Further, as a percentage of the school roll, the proportions of children in each of these language groups was similar, see Table 9.

2.22 There was a higher proportion of inner city schools with children whose first language was not English. Seven out of ten inner city schools had some such children compared with four out of ten in 'other urban' areas and one out of ten in rural areas. Half of the inner city schools had 3 per cent or more children whose first language was not English compared with one out of five in 'other urban' areas. There were virtually no schools with these proportions of such children in rural areas.

2.23 Although inner city schools were more likely than others to have pupils for whom English was a second language, many of these children were in inner city schools which were not classified as being in areas of

---

[1]See Chapter 2 paragraph 7.

marked social disadvantage, see Table 10. The need to contend with pupils for whom English is a second language is therefore not only or even especially a matter for schools in areas of marked social difficulty.

2.24 Children whose first language was English but who had predominantly West Indian speech patterns were a special consideration in some schools. Six per cent of the schools had some children in this category although less than 1 per cent of the schools had more than one in fifty such children on roll. Of course, children from indigenous families also vary in their use of English, see Table 11.

2.25 Provision was made for many pupils who lacked facility in the English language through the normal arrangements for remedial teaching within the school[1]. Some children attended special language centres and occasionally such provision was made within the schools. There were too few schools involved in this work for formal analysis to show what standards were achieved compared with average levels of performance in the whole sample, but the following examples indicate the kind of practices which were observed :

'Approaching half of the school population is of overseas origin. These are mainly children born in this country, but whose families may not speak English at home. Children with a poor command of the English language attend an infant language centre before admission to school at about $5\frac{1}{2}$ to 6 years of age ; no further specialised language teaching is given although the arrangements for remedial reading provide opportunities for conversation in small groups.'

'The teacher of English as a second language worked in the school each morning. She took five or six children at a time grouped according to their home language and not necessarily by their competence in English. The room in which the teaching took place was a microcosm of the school as a whole. The children contributed to display materials from their home cultures and there were examples of the full range of primary school work done in the room. The English the children were learning was based on the work done in the children's ordinary classes as well as on their lives outside school. The different levels of competence in English within a group were well used to encourage learning and teaching between the children as well as between teacher and child. Although conversation was the principal means of communica-

---

[1] See Annex to Chapter 3, Table 17.

tion, reading and writing, including the writing of figures and use of numbers, also played a prominent part. Classes were arranged after school for mothers who wished to learn English.'

Annex to Chapter 2

All the data in the tables are weighted.[1]

Schools:	weighted sample size = 300
	actual sample size = 540
7 year old classes:	weighted sample size = 480
	actual sample size = 404
9 year old classes:	weighted sample size = 424
	actual sample size = 373
11 year old classes:	weighted sample size = 365
	actual sample size = 344

Percentages in the tables are rounded.

The numbers are weighted and rounded. They do not necessarily add up to the weighted total.

Weighting

Schools did not all have the same chance of being selected for the sample. The same is true for classes. The reasons for this, which are complex, are discussed in Appendix B. Weighting is the technique of compensating for these unequal selection probabilities.[2] Unequal selection probabilities and weighting offered advantages[3] and were all part of the sample design. The weighted sample size is the total on which a table is based. The actual sample size is the number of schools or classes actually sampled.

---

[1] See Appendix D.
[2] See Appendix D.
[3] See Appendix B.

Table 1. *The percentage of schools of each organisational type falling within the different localities.*

	Infant	Junior	Junior with infant	First
Inner City	24	19	13	17
'Other urban'	63	69	26	52
Rural	14	12	61	32
Total %	100	100	100	100

Table 2. *The percentage of schools of each organisational type shown by form entry*[1] (*size of year group*).

	Infant	Junior	Junior with infant	First
One-form entry or smaller	9	9	67	37
Two-form entry	51	48	31	42
Three-form entry or larger	40	44	2	21
Total %	100	100	100	100

Note The number of combined and middle schools in the sample was too small to produce reliable percentages.

[1] See Appendix B for definition of form entry.

Table 3 The percentage of schools of each organisational type within different localities shown by form entry (fe) (size of year group)

Type of School	Inner city				'Other urban'				Rural				All localities			
	1fe	2fe	3fe	Total	1fe	2fe	3fe	Total	1fe	2fe	3fe	Total	1fe	2fe	3fe	Total
Infant	–	17	11	28	3	13	12	27	1	4	2	7	2	10	8	19
Junior	–	14	8	22	2	13	14	30	2	3	2	6	2	9	8	19
Junior with infant	16	20	1	37	9	18	2	29	67	10	*	77	33	15	1	49
First	4	4	3	11	2	7	3	12	7	1	1	9	4	4	2	11
First with middle	–	2	–	2	1	1	–	2	1	1	–	2	1	1	–	2
Percentage of all schools in the locality	20	57	23	100	17	52	31	100	77	19	5	100	42	39	19	100

*Less than 0.5%

Note: Percentages for first with middle schools are not reliable because of the small number of such schools in the sample

Table 4   The percentages of men and women class teachers of the survey classes

	7 year old classes	9 year old classes	11 year old classes
Men	3	30	49
Women	97	70	51
Total %	100	100	100

Table 5   Percentage of graduate and non-graduate teachers by total teaching experience in the survey schools

	BEd	Other graduates	Non-graduates	Total %
Less than 1 year	13	8	79	100
1 up to 5 years	8	6	86	100
5 up to 15 years	3	7	90	100
15 years or more	1	5	94	100
All teachers	4	6	90	100

Note :   Measurement was on the basis of the number of completed terms. Hence less than one year implies two or fewer completed terms

Table 6   The percentages of teachers of the survey classes by phase of initial training

	7 year old classes	9 year old classes	11 year old classes
Nursery/infant	14	0	4
Infant	15	2	2
First	5	0	0
Infant/junior	45	15	15
Junior	12	40	35
Junior/secondary	5	37	25
Middle	0	3	2
Secondary	2	2	13
Other	2	2	2
Total %	100	100	100
% teaching an age group for which initially trained	79	95	77

Table 7 The percentage of men and women teachers in the survey schools by salary scale

Salary scale	Men	Women	All teachers
Scale 1	3	37	40
Scale 2	6	29	35
Scale 3	2	3	5
Scale 4	*	*	*
Deputy	2	7	9
Heads	6	5	11
Total %	19	81	100

*Less than 5%

Notes: Weighted sample size (men) 594 Actual sample size (men) 1185

Weighted sample size (women) 2252 Actual sample size (women) 4659

Table 8 The percentage of schools having teachers (excluding head teachers) with organisational responsibilities by form of entry (size of year group)

	% of one-form entry or smaller schools	% of two-form entry schools	% of three-form entry or larger schools	% of all schools
Library	30	72	69	54
Infant department	55 (60)	42 (83)	10 (60)	41 (67)
Remedial work	22	49	58	38
Resource centre	12	36	45	28
Year group leader	4	17	40	16
Junior department	11 (7)	21 (44)	7 (40)	14 (20)
Liaison with other schools	3	16	29	13
Team leader	7	14	27	13
Home/school liaison	4	16	20	12
Nursery unit	8	14	15	12
Needs of the very able	–	4	4	2
Others	23	52	61	41

Notes: Where a school had more than one teacher with a particular responsibility the school is counted only once.

The teachers shown are not necessarily on above Scale 1 posts.

The figure in brackets in the table show the percentage for combined infant with junior schools and first with middle schools.

Table 9 The percentage of schools having children for whom English is a second language

Percentages of children on roll for whom English is a second language	First language of Indian or Pakistani origin	First language of European origin other than English	First language of African origin	First language of Chinese origin	All first languages other than English
None on roll	80	82	94	90	67
Up to 2% on roll	10	11	5	8	16
3 to 5% on roll	3	3	1	2	6
6 to 10% on roll	2	2	None	None	3
11 to 15% on roll	2	1	None	None	3
16 to 50% on roll	3	1	None	None	4
51% or more on roll	None	None	None	None	1
All schools %	100	100	100	100	100

Note: This information was supplied by schools rounded up to the next whole per cent.

17

Table 10 The percentage of schools by area of marked social difficulty, locality and the percentage of children on roll for whom English is a second language

Percentage of children on roll for whom English is a second language	Inner city			'Other urban'			Rural			All localities		
	Marked social difficulty	Not marked social difficulty	Total	Marked social difficulty	Not marked social difficulty	Total	Marked social difficulty	Not marked social difficulty	Total	Marked social difficulty	Not marked social difficulty	Total
None on role	25	32	28	54	58	58	88[1]	93	91	45	71	67
Up to 2%	25	18	22	21	23	23	12[1]	6	7	22	15	16
More than 2%	50	50	50	25	19	20	–[1]	1	1	33	14	17
Total %	100	100	100	100	100	100	100	100	100	100	100	100
Total number (weighted)	28	22	50	24	110	133	8	109	117	59	241	300
Total number (unweighted)	55	46	101	54	235	289	10	140	150	119	421	540

[1] These percentages are given for completeness. They are based on only eight schools and therefore must be considered as very approximate.

Note: This information was supplied by schools rounded up to the next whole per cent.

Table 11 The percentage of schools having children with predominantly West Indian speech patterns

Percentage on roll	None	2 or less	3–5	6–10	11 or more	All schools
Percentage of schools	94	5	1	–	–	100

Note: This information was supplied by schools as a percentage rounded up to the next whole per cent.

3 The classes: organisation and arrangements affecting children's work

i. ORGANISATION OF CLASSES

3.1 The ages of the children are always an important factor to take into account when arranging children in their classes. One practice, commonly adopted, is to arrange each class so that it contains children born during one school year and, if the school is large enough, there may be two or more classes in each year group. Some schools, though apparently large enough to arrange classes in year groups, have classes with mixed age groups. Other schools are small and have to combine children from two or more age groups in order to form each class. Figure 6 in the Annex to Chapter 2 shows how common these three kinds of class arrangements were in the survey schools.

3.2 The schools that were apparently large enough to form classes of one age group but did not do so fell into three categories. Some had classes with a majority of children from one school year group and a small number from another age group. Generally these were schools where the year groups were more than ordinarily uneven and the mixture of age groups made it possible to even the sizes of the classes. In the second category were schools which had classes with a substantial number of children from each of two age groups. The remainder were schools which had classes with a substantial number of children from each of three or more age groups. Classes in these last two categories are usually referred to as vertically grouped classes; they may be the result of organisational convenience or of a deliberate policy decision within the school. A system of vertically grouped classes is sometimes adopted in infant schools and departments to avoid the necessity of moving children to a new class during the course of the school year. Such moves are more likely when new children are admitted to school at the beginning of the spring or summer term as well as at the beginning of the school year. The incidence of 'mixed age' classes is shown in Figure 7 in the Annex to Chapter 2.

Figure 6 Arrangement of children in the survey classes: (a) classes arranged in single age school year groups; (b) classes arranged as mixed age classes where schools were too small to allow single age school year groups; (c) classes arranged as mixed age classes where schools were large enough to allow single age school year groups.

Figure 7 Arrangement of children in classes where schools were large enough to allow single age school year groups but chose not to: (a) majority of children of one school year group with a few of a different age; (b) children from two school year groups with significant numbers from both age groups; (c) children from three or more school year groups with significant numbers from at least three age groups.

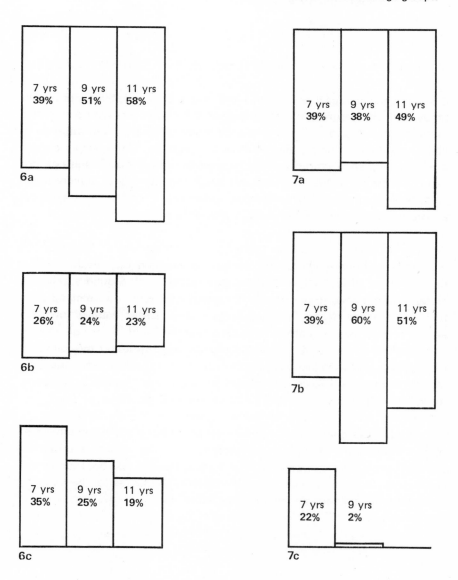

3.3 In very few schools were classes streamed according to ability. About a third of schools were large enough to be in a position to stream, and of these less than a fifth did so. Younger children were the least likely to be in streamed classes and only about one in twenty classes of 11 year olds was streamed, see Table 12 in the Annex to this Chapter.

3.4 Some schools arrange small permanent classes for children who find learning difficult. These classes were not included among those inspected for the purposes of this survey.

ii. CLASSROOM ARRANGEMENTS IN THE SURVEY CLASSES

3.5 Since the classes in the survey were mainly of mixed ability, and sometimes vertically grouped, it is to be expected that teachers would employ a range of methods to cater for the wide range of abilities and interests of children within a single class. Most of the teachers in the survey classes grouped children in various ways for some part of their work. These groups varied according to the subject being taught or the kind of activity being undertaken and were usually formed or reformed for particular purposes or according to the needs of the moment, see Table 13.

3.6 The grouping of children within a class according to their abilities occurred most frequently for the teaching of mathematics; in this subject the sequence of learning is fairly clearly defined and teachers generally recognised the need to present children with tasks which were matched to their competence. Nearly three-quarters of the classes were grouped by ability for their work in mathematics. Over half the 9 and 11 year old classes and nearly two-thirds of 7 year old classes were grouped by ability for reading and, in fewer classes, for writing. In these aspects of language work readily identifiable skills are being taught and teachers are clearly concerned to present children with tasks at the right level of difficulty.

3.7 Children were rarely grouped by ability for their work in any other area of the curriculum. Individual assignments of work, whether presented directly by the teacher, from a graded reading book, a text book or a work card, were also used in a considerable majority of classes for the teaching of reading, writing and mathematics, see Table 14.

Figure 8 The percentage of all classes grouped by ability for mathematics, reading and writing

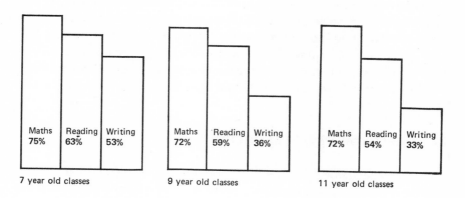

| Maths 75% | Reading 63% | Writing 53% | Maths 72% | Reading 59% | Writing 36% | Maths 72% | Reading 54% | Writing 33% |

7 year old classes   9 year old classes   11 year old classes

3.8 Mixed ability, 'shared interest' or 'friendship' groups were most commonly used in the teaching of art and craft, physical education and science, see Table 15. In these subjects a range of specialised materials, apparatus and equipment is used. This often leads to the adoption of a type of organisation which allows different activities to take place at the same time within a shared working space whether in the hall, classroom or elsewhere; this makes it possible to employ a wider range but a smaller quantity of apparatus or materials than if every child has to have equipment of a similar type at the same time. Boys and girls were not usually separated for any aspect of their work in 7 year old classes. In 9 and 11 year old classes some separation occurred for craft and physical education[1].

3.9 About half the classes in the survey regrouped with other classes for some part of their work. In the case of 9 and 11 year old classes this occurred most frequently for music, craft and physical education where access to specialised equipment or to areas such as playing fields or swimming baths was essential and, in some cases, these arrangements enabled some exchange of teachers to take place. Seven year old classes were regrouped less often than the older children, mainly for music and language work. This probably reflects the occasions when vertically grouped classes were re-formed so that children of about the same age could be drawn together for storytelling and discussion and also when classes combined for singing or for a story session, see Table 16.

---

[1]See Chapter 5 v, paragraphs 95 and 105.

3.10 A variety of arrangements was adopted to help the less able children, the most common being the withdrawal of individuals or groups of children to work with another teacher. In a fifth of the classes cooperative working by the teachers enabled the regrouping of two or more classes to take place and special attention to be given to the less able pupils. This method also occasionally enabled some teachers to give particular attention to groups of the exceptionally able children ; these pupils were rarely withdrawn from the normal class to be given special help, see Table 17.

iii. DEPLOYMENT OF TEACHERS

3.11 The arrangement whereby a class teacher is responsible for the teaching of the whole, or the major part of, the curriculum of his or her class is often regarded as the traditional form of organisation for teaching in the primary school. This form of organisation undoubtedly makes heavy demands on the individual teacher, particularly as children grow older and their learning covers a wider and deeper range of knowledge and skills in all areas of the curriculum.

3.12 Over three-quarters of all the classes in the survey were taught for some of the time by teachers other than their own class teacher, excluding peripatetic teachers. The oldest children were the most likely to be taught by other teachers, particularly for music, physical education and English language. The proportion of classes taught by three or more other teachers also increased with the age of the pupils. A third of 9 year old and two-fifths of 11 year old classes were taught by three or more teachers in addition to the class teacher, see Table 18.

3.13 Peripatetic teachers[1] worked with children in nearly half the 11 year old classes and in two-fifths of 9 year old classes ; for the most part they taught individual children or small groups to play stringed instruments, or took small groups of children or individuals for reading tuition, see Table 19.

3.14 While the majority of classes were taught for at least some of their time by teachers other than their own class teacher, the range of work for which this provision was made was mainly limited to music, English language and physical education, see Table 20. More than a third of 7 year

---

[1]The data on peripatetic teachers are based on part of the sample only. See Annex A Section 6 Paragraph 4.

Figure 9 The percentage of classes visited by peripatetic teachers

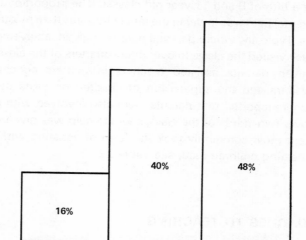

16%	40%	48%
7 yr old classes	9 yr old classes	11 yr old classes

old classes and over half the 9 and 11 year old classes were taught by another teacher for music and about a third of the older classes were taken for physical education by another teacher. A quarter of 7 year old classes were taught only by their own class teachers. Children were rarely taught by another teacher for a period exceeding five hours during the course of a week; even at 11 years over a third of the classes were taught for less than two hours a week by a teacher other than their own class teacher, see Table 21.

iv. ADDITIONAL ADULT HELP

3.15 Non-teaching paid adult helpers assisted teachers in just over half of the 7 year old classes in the survey. About a fifth of 9 and 11 year old classes also received this kind of support, see Table 22. About a fifth of the 7 year old classes received such help for 6 hours or more per week while nearly half 9 and 11 year old classes received less than one hour. At all three ages, but particularly in classes of 7 year olds, schools in 'other urban' areas did not receive as much assistance as schools in inner city and rural areas.

3.16 Parents helped teachers in nearly a third of the 7 year old classes and in just under a fifth of 9 and 11 year old classes. The proportion of classes receiving parental help was lower in the inner city areas than in 'other urban' or rural areas. Typically, where parental help was given, an average of two parents a week visited the class. In over three-quarters of the classes where help was given parents assisted teachers in matters concerning the children's welfare and the supervision of children on visits outside the school. Teachers reported that parents were also involved with children's learning in over two-thirds of the classes where help was given. This type of involvement most commonly took the form of assisting with practical subjects or hearing children read, see Table 23.

v. APPROACHES TO TEACHING

3.17 A quiet working atmosphere was established in nine out of ten of the classes whenever it was needed.

3.18 It is clear from the evidence that a variety of types of organisation was used in arranging the work of the classes. Generally, the organisation was designed to provide satisfactorily for children of different attainments and abilities, to accommodate various types of work, including practical work, and to take advantage of the resources and teaching strengths available within a particular school.

3.19 Teachers also varied their own approach to teaching according to the circumstances, and in the course of one lesson a variety of approaches might be used. For this reason it can be misleading to categorise teaching methods. Nevertheless, for the purpose of this survey two broad approaches to teaching were postulated. They were defined as 'mainly didactic' and 'mainly exploratory'. A didactic approach was one in which the teacher directed the children's work in accordance with relatively specific and predetermined intentions and where explanations usually, though not always, preceded the action taken by the children. An exploratory approach was one in which the broad objectives of the work were discussed with the children but where they were then put in a position of finding their own solutions to the problems posed and of making choices about the way in which the work should be tackled. The scope and timescale of the tasks involved were likely to be flexible and the path of the work was likely to be modified in the light of events; explanation by the teacher more often accompanied or followed action taken by the children.

3.20 In the survey classes about three-quarters of the teachers employed a mainly didactic approach, while less than one in twenty relied mainly on an exploratory approach. In about one-fifth of the classes teachers employed an appropriate combination of didactic and exploratory methods, varying their approach according to the nature of the task in hand, and could not be said to incline to either approach.

3.21 In only about one class in twenty was too little guidance given to children about what they should be doing. When this occurred children were uncertain of what was required and this could lead to aimless activity and lack of progress. In the majority of classes, however, the content of children's work and their use of resources was prescribed, sometimes to the extent that there was insufficient opportunity for the children to incorporate information and ideas of their own or to make use of spontaneous incidents which arose.

3.22 The impetus for extended studies which involved children over a period of time could arise from the children or be introduced by the teacher. An example of the former arose in an 11 year old class where a boy's interest in butterflies and moths began when his class was taken out to study a meadow. The boy used a sweep net to catch and examine insects and other small animals living in the long grass. Among the creatures he caught were two meadow brown moths and he noticed their colouring was not identical. This led him to look for colour variation among other butterflies and moths, to examine wing scales under a microscope and to rear caterpillars found on some nettles. During this work the boy referred to several books to help him with identification of species, kept careful notes and made detailed drawings of all he saw. Subsequently, the teacher acquired some eggs of the Assam moth and the boy reared them successfully, having the satisfaction of seeing one imago emerge from a pupa.

3.23 Evidence of this kind of work was available in about one class in ten. A good example of an extended study by a group of children, introduced by the teacher, was seen in a 7 year old class where the teacher had introduced a topic on water, following the interest aroused in the children by a burst water main outside the school gate. In the course of the work, children examined a number of different aspects of the subject including rusting, floating, sinking, water levels, rates of flow, the importance of water to plant and animal life, and where their own supply of drinking water came from. The work involved discussion, writing, drawing and practical experiment, and culminated in a visit to a local reservoir.

3.24 In this case the teacher used a combination of didactic and exploratory approaches, sometimes introducing the work with discussion and explanation, occasionally following up a point of interest raised by a child and sometimes presenting the children with a practical problem to be investigated. The problems posed were usually specific and pre-determined, concerned, for example, with the investigation of properties of corrosibility and buoyancy or the effects of water pressure; explanations preceded, accompanied or followed the children's activities, with the teacher varying her approaches according to the needs of the moment.

Annex to Chapter 3

All the data in the tables are weighted[1].

Table 12 The incidence of streaming by ability in the survey schools

	7 year old classes	9 year old classes	11 year old classes
% of all schools where streaming is not possible (one-form entry or less)	62	63	67
% of all schools where streaming is possible	38	37	33
Total %	100	100	100
Of those schools where streaming was possible % which streamed	3	10	17
Of all schools in the survey % which streamed	1	4	6

[1] See Appendix D

Table 13 The patterns of grouping adopted within the survey classes

	7 year old classes	9 year old classes	11 year old classes
Of all classes % using groups	96	96	97
Of those classes which used groups :			
% using groups regularly, arranged according to subjects being taught	45	40	38
% not normally grouped but groups sometimes formed according to the needs of the moment	41	54	53
% using same groups for all subjects	14	6	9
Total %	100	100	100

Table 14 Percentage of classes using individual assignments of work

	7 year old classes			9 year old classes			11 year old classes		
% of all classes using individual assignments for any subject	84			89			92		
% of all classes using individual assignments for the following:	Frequently	Occasion-ally	Never	Frequently	Occasion-ally	Never	Frequently	Occasion-ally	Never
Reading	75	7	18	75	8	17	72	12	16
Writing	69	13	18	65	18	17	66	22	12
Mathematics	67	15	18	52	29	19	51	33	16
Art	50	24	26	42	33	25	46	33	21
Crafts	49	25	26	43	33	24	48	32	20
Social Studies	13	25	62	28	33	39	38	31	31

Note: Only areas of the curriculum where individual assignments were used in more than two-fifths of classes are shown

Table 15 Characteristics used for grouping children for work in individual subjects for all classes

% of all classes grouped for		7 year old classes	9 year old classes	11 year old classes
MATHEMATICS by:				
	Ability	75	72	72
	Mixed ability	6	8	8
	Other	9	5	4
	Total %	90	85	85
READING by:				
	Ability	63	59	54
	Mixed ability	5	7	9
	Other	4	3	2
	Total %	72	69	65
WRITING by:				
	Ability	53	36	33
	Mixed ability	10	10	13
	Other	10	7	7
	Total %	73	53	53
ART and CRAFT by:				
	Ability	2	2	1
	Mixed ability	17	12	15
	Other	28	31	24
	Total %	47	45	40
PHYSICAL EDUCATION by:				
	Ability	1	1	1
	Mixed ability	26	32	29
	Other	10	18	20
	Total %	37	51	50
SCIENCE by:				
	Ability	4	3	4
	Mixed ability	10	15	18
	Other	11	18	19
	Total %	25	36	41

Notes: Where more than one characteristic was used only the dominant characteristic is shown.

Only subjects where grouping was used in more than 25 per cent of classes in each age group is shown.

'Other' criteria include shared interest and friendship groups.

Table 16 The incidence of regrouping with other classes

	7 year old classes		9 year old classes		11 year old classes	
% of all classes regrouping with other classes	35		48		56	
Subjects for which classes are most commonly regrouped and percentage of all classes affected	Music	24	Music	27	Craft	32
	Language work:		Craft	25	Physical education	32
	(a) Listening	20	Physical education	23	Music	29
	(b) Talking	17				

Note: In no other subjects was regrouping used with anything like the same frequency as those named above

Table 17 Patterns of school organisation designed to cater for less able and exceptionally able children

	7 year old classes	9 year old classes	11 year old classes
LESS ABLE CHILDREN			
% of all classes affected by:			
Withdrawal of groups	43	53	52
Withdrawal of individuals	41	52	47
Cooperative working by teachers	20	20	20
Supernumerary teacher in the class	12	8	9
Long-term withdrawal to a special class	2	6	7
EXCEPTIONALLY ABLE CHILDREN			
% of all classes affected by:			
Withdrawal of groups	9	4	8
Withdrawal of individuals	3	1	2
Cooperative working by teachers	7	7	11
Supernumerary teacher in the class	3	2	1
Long-term withdrawal to a special class	—	—	*

*Less than 0.5%

Table 18 Percentage of classes taught by teachers other than own class teacher

	7 year old	9 year old	11 year old
% of all classes taught by other teachers	73	85	90
Of the above classes % taught by the following number of other teachers: 1	48	33	25
2	31	35	32
3	16	20	20
4	3	7	15
5	2	4	6
6 or more	—	1	2
Total %	100	100	100

Table 19 Percentage of all classes with children taught by peripatetic teachers for reading and stringed instruments

	7 year old classes	9 year old classes	11 year old classes
Reading	7	19	17
Stringed instruments	2	19	25

Note: The data on peripatetic teachers is based on part of the sample only.
(See Annex A, section 6, paragraph 4)

Table 20 Percentage of classes taught by teacher other than own class teacher by subjects

%	7 year old classes		9 year old classes		11 year old classes
40	Music	50	Music	55	Music
30	Language	35	Language	40	Physical education
10	Physical education	30	Physical education	30	Language
	Art and craft				Art and craft
5	Mathematics	20	Art and craft	20	French
		10	Mathematics	10	Science
					Mathematics
		5	French		
			Science		

Note: Percentages rounded to nearest 5

Table 21 Percentage of classes taught for given number of hours per week by teachers other than own class teacher

Number of hours per week	7 year old classes	9 year old classes	11 year old classes
None	26	14	10
Up to 2 hours	45	35	27
2 up to 5 hours	25	42	46
5 up to 10 hours	3	7	13
10 or more hours	1	2	4
Total %	100	100	100

Table 22 Percentage of classes receiving non-teaching paid adult help

	7 year old classes	9 year old classes	11 year old classes
% of all classes with one or more helpers	56	23	19
Of the above classes % with the following number of helpers:			
1	84	91	95
2	14	9	5
3	2	–	–
Total %	100	100	100

Table 23 Percentage of classes receiving voluntary parental help and the activities undertaken

	7 year old classes	9 year old classes	11 year old classes
Of all classes % receiving parental help	31	18	17
Of those classes where help was given % in which it included :			
children's welfare, including school visits	83	76	78
involvement with children's learning	66	64	71
preparing materials and resources	59	36	41
other kinds of involvement	52	54	61

4 The curriculum: planning and continuity

i. TEACHERS WITH SPECIAL CURRICULAR RESPONSIBILITIES

4.1 Heads and teachers are responsible for seeing that the curriculum of their school is appropriately covered both within individual classes and throughout the school. The programme of work planned for the children must take into account the subject matter to be taught and the means of helping children to learn, understand and make progress. The effectiveness of such a programme can be considerably enhanced if individual teachers are given responsibility within the school for both the planning and oversight of the work in relation to particular aspects of the curriculum. The allocation of responsibilities for subjects within the curriculum was often associated with the award of scale 2 or higher posts although this was not always the case, see Table 24.

4.2 The way in which positions of responsibility for areas of the curriculum were distributed no doubt reflected a variety of factors, not least the size of the school and the number of posts available. Responsibility for music was recognised in 70 per cent of all the schools. This is a subject in which many teachers feel they do not have sufficient expertise and was one of the subjects most frequently taught by a teacher other than the class teacher[1]. The wish to attract a competent musician to the staff of a school probably accounts, in part, for the frequency with which special posts had been allocated to music.

4.3 Overall responsibility for the work in English language, including reading, was allocated to a named teacher in half of all the schools, although in two form entry schools the teaching of games was more frequently listed than language work. Taken together, posts of responsibility for games, swimming and gymnastics formed a very substantial group. It may be that

---

[1] See Annex to Chapter 3, Table 20

the number of posts allocated for games and swimming reflected the additional organisational duties often associated with these subjects.

4.4 Posts with special responsibility for games were more common than posts for mathematics, except in three form entry and larger schools where mathematics ranked second only to music. Posts for science occurred in less than a fifth of schools and were also, proportionally, more frequently represented in the larger schools. Responsibility for art and crafts was allocated in about a third of all the schools.

4.5 In a quarter of the schools in the survey teachers with positions of curricular or organisational responsibility were having a noticeable influence on the quality of work in the school as a whole. In the remaining schools there was little evidence that the influence of teachers with curricular responsibilities spread beyond the work in their own classes. Where teachers with responsibilities for a particular area of the curriculum were effective in influencing the work of the school this was apparent in a number of ways: in the case of English language and mathematics there was evidence of teachers planning programmes of work in consultation with the head, advising other teachers and helping to encourage a consistent approach to the work in these subjects.

4.6 To some extent such an approach was reflected in the fact that 85 per cent or more of schools had schemes of work in mathematics and English. Nearly three-quarters of the schools had written guidelines for religious education; in all local authorities 'agreed syllabuses' are provided and in county and controlled schools the schemes are adapted from these. In any other subject fewer than half of the schools had a scheme of work, see Table 25. There was evidence in the survey that where a teacher with a special responsibility was able to exercise it through the planning and supervision of a programme of work, this was effective in raising the standards of work and the levels of expectation of what children were capable of doing[1].

ii. TRANSITION BETWEEN CLASSES

4.7 The 7, 9 and 11 year olds had almost all previously been in another class within the same school. The teachers indicated that a variety of

---

[1] See Chapter 7, paragraphs 36 and 37 and Note 12

methods were used to assess the capabilities of the children when they arrived in their new classes. Most of the class teachers were able to hold discussions with the children's previous teacher and nearly half had visited the children in their former classes. Three-quarters of the teachers indicated that they were able to refer to the school's records on the progress of individual children and in over a third of the classes teachers received individual folders containing samples of each child's work. The use of individual folders of work was more common in the infant classes than in the classes containing junior children. Tests devised by the school were considerably more likely to be given to children in the 9 and 11 year old classes, see Table 26.

4.8 The use of commercially produced standardised tests is a method of comparing the attainment of individual children, or classes, with others of their age in a large number of schools. Over four-fifths of the 9 and 11 year old classes and nearly half of the 7 year old classes used standardised tests to monitor children's progress; more than a third of the 9 and 11 year old classes used published tests for diagnostic purposes.

iii. CONTINUITY BETWEEN SCHOOLS

4.9 Various measures were used to ease the transition of children between schools. The majority of schools maintained some form of record of the progress of individual children. Four fifths of the schools used official local education authority records and three-fifths had devised their own system of record keeping, often in addition to the official record. Separate infant and larger schools were more likely to provide their own system of record keeping. About a fifth of the schools kept individual folders of work samples to accompany the child to his next school.

4.10 In over four-fifths of the schools heads, and occasionally other teachers, were able to visit the schools to which children would be transferring and in over 90 per cent of the schools the children visited their future school before the transition took place. Half of the schools received information on the subsequent progress of the children in their new schools, see Table 27.

4.11 Joint meetings of teachers from the contributory and receiving schools for discussion about the curriculum took place in less than a third of the schools. While considerable efforts were clearly made to ease children's transition from one school to the next, the importance of continuity in the curriculum of the schools was largely overlooked. The planning of the curriculum and the preparation of schemes of work should take into account the requirements of the next stage of education as well as the effects of the previous stage. This can be achieved only if there is regular and systematic consultation between teachers from the associated schools.

Annex to Chapter 4

All the data in the tables are weighted[1].

Table 24 The percentage of schools having teachers with special curricular responsibilities by form of entry (size of year group)

	% of one-form entry schools or smaller	% of two-form entry schools	% of three-form entry schools or larger	% of all schools
Music	55	78	84	70
Language (including reading)	37	58	63	51
Games	32	63	51	48
Mathematics	31	49	65	45
Craft	20	40	52	35
Swimming	27	36	35	32
Art	13	36	57	31
Gymnastics	10	33	37	25
Religious education	17	23	18	19
Science	8	20	30	17
Environmental studies	9	20	27	17
Drama	6	19	20	14
French	12	16	14	14
Dance	8	16	18	13

Notes : No other subject was represented in more than 4% of all schools

Where a school had more than one teacher responsible for a particular subject the school is counted only once for that subject

The teachers concerned do not necessarily hold posts above Scale 1

[1] See Appendix D

Table 25 The percentage of schools with written guidelines or schemes of work for each subject

Subject	% of schools	Subject	% of schools	Subject	% of schools
Mathematics	88	Music	37	Social studies	18
Language	85	History	36	Dance	17
Religious education	72	Geography	35	Health education	17
Science	43	Environmental studies	34	French	15
Art	42	Games	26	Humanities	9
Craft	41	Swimming	19	Other subjects	17
Gymnastics	38	Drama	18		

Table 26 Methods used by class teachers to assess children's capabilities on arrival in a new class

Methods	% of classes using method		
	7 year old classes	9 year old classes	11 year old classes
Discussion with previous teacher	86	93	95
Schools' individual records	74	79	76
Children visited in previous class	44	43	46
Class lists of marks or positions	37	53	55
Folders of work samples	43	32	29
School tests	14	41	45

Table 27 Measures most frequently used to ease transfer between schools

Measures used to ease transfer	% of schools
Visits by children before transfer	92
Occasional visits by teachers	83
Visits by heads	82
Information on subsequent progress	50
Joint meetings of teachers for discussion about the curriculum	29
Regular visits by teachers	10

5 The content of the curriculum

i. SKILLS AND ATTITUDES

5.1 In Sections ii to vi of this chapter the curriculum is discussed in terms of subjects such as English, mathematics or geography, or in relation to certain activities such as learning to read or to play team games. Many of the skills, ideas and attitudes referred to have applications that recur in various parts of school work, but they also need to be taught quite specifically and time has to be given, for example, to teaching children to calculate and to read. Because this kind of teaching is not wholly susceptible to fixed timetable periods many classes have broadly drawn timetables with times specified only when resources or specialist teachers are shared among a number of classes.

5.2 The advantages that can come from improving language skills and developing ideas by applying them widely in many areas of the curriculum were discussed in the Bullock Report. The same general principle applies to some other aspects of learning, and examples were found in a number of schools. Music was ordinarily played or sung during the daily act of worship, and it was fairly common for children to accompany the hymn or to play a piece on the musical instruments they were learning; this required careful preparation and practice and also provided motivation. Drama was used on occasions to bring a bible story to life, or to highlight a historical incident.

5.3 These uses of one activity to promote learning in connection with another could be considerably extended. This was particularly so in such basic skills as calculating and measuring which were seldom applied to work on historical, geographical or even scientific topics. Similarly, more could be done, particulraly with the older children, to encourage them to follow a line of argument, to evaluate evidence and alternative points of view, or to reach judgments in the course of discussion, and in their own writing.

5.4 There were notable occasions when children were seen to be required to think things through, as, for example, in the 11 year old class which was mapping the course of a river near their school. The children followed a small tributary which disappeared underground and the teacher asked the children to think about where it might have gone. This led to a careful examination of the surrounding area and the contours of the land. The children produced a number of possible alternatives and subsequently put forward arguments suggesting which was the most likely course, with some pupils producing evidence to support their different points of view. While the course of the tributary was not finally discovered, the children had valuable experience in presenting their cases and marshalling evidence to support them.

Social and moral learning

5.5 Some aspects of learning are so general that they rarely appear as subject or timetable headings. Social development and moral learning include essential elements of this kind, yet were aspects of children's development frequently given attention in the course of the day to day work in every classroom.

5.6 Heads were asked to state briefly in writing what their schools set out in social and moral education. Their replies confirm the view that, in most primary schools, living and working together amicably and successfully is given high priority. The schools in the survey attached particular importance to children acquiring a sense of social responsibility, whether by performing tasks related to the general welfare of the school or class, or through the way work was arranged and carried out in the classroom. In nine out of ten classes teachers provided planned opportunities for children to take responsibility and to participate as members of a group or team. The older children particularly were also given opportunities to exercise leadership.

5.7 Consideration for other people and concern for the natural environment and for living creatures was widely encouraged. In almost all the classes children were taught to respect their surroundings and were expected to take care of materials, equipment and other objects in the classroom and the school generally. The widespread use of groups in the arrangements for teaching[1] provided many opportunities for children to be taught to behave in a responsible and considerate way. In about two-thirds of the

[1] See Annex to Chapter 3, Table 13

classes there was evidence of situations being planned and used to encourage children to make informed choices, to use their initiative and to be responsible for their own work and behaviour.

5.8 In a similar number of classes teachers helped children to become aware of their own feelings and emotions by making use of incidental situations which arose; for example, by helping an individual child to understand why he had behaved aggressively or selfishly or by helping other children to understand and be tolerant. One teacher of an 11 year old class followed a rather violent classroom quarrel by the introduction of a story which aroused lively discussion and helped the whole group, and in particular the two boys concerned in the quarrel, to understand what had happened and why they had become angry.

5.9 The evidence of this survey suggests that as long as teachers continue to be aware of the importance of social and moral learning there is much to be said for an approach which takes advantage of opportunities that arise throughout the school day and are related to work within any part of the curriculum.

Learning to notice and to think

5.10 There is hardly any aspect of the curriculum in which children can make progress without taking careful notice of what they see, hear or otherwise experience, and without thinking about their observations.

5.11 In learning the basic skills of reading children are required to listen carefully, to notice similarities and differences in sounds and in shapes of letters, to generalise about the ways in which visual symbols represent sounds, words and meanings, to classify groups of letters as they relate to sounds and to notice and remember exceptions to general rules.

5.12 Opportunities for discriminating, classifying and observing inter-relations arise in connection with work in all areas of the curriculum. They could be used more fully than they are.

5.13 In art children rarely drew or painted from careful and detailed observation of things around them; accurate and careful measurement and observation were seldom a part of the work in science, craft or social studies. Whether they are working at first-hand or with secondary sources children need help in noticing relevant features and generalising from their observations. Specially devised activities to support practice in classifying and generalising, for example, exercises involving the manipulation of coloured shapes, may have a useful place but they are a poor substitute for the varied and interesting work with plants, animals and all kinds of natural and man-made materials and objects, through which these cognitive skills are, in a minority of schools, developed in the various parts of the curriculum.

Recording and practical skills

5.14 Writing, drawing and painting were the forms of recording most frequently used in the majority of the classes in the survey. While four-fifths of all the classes made some use of graphical and other diagrammatic forms of presentation in mathematics, there was little evidence that children were encouraged to employ these methods to present their work in other areas of the curriculum. The use and making of maps and plans was given little attention even in relation to geographical aspects of the work. Three dimensional models were used to illustrate work in geography and history, but older children, particularly, had few opportunities for constructional work with resistant materials which required accuracy and precision. Tools and equipment to assist more precise construction, measurement and observation were seldom available for work in craft or science.

5.15 Techniques learned in mathematics were infrequently used in other areas of the curriculum or related to everyday situations, and children were seldom required to quantify as part of their recording, except in mathematics lessons. While particular computational techniques have to be taught and practised there is considerable advantage in children appreciating their application in a wide context.

5.16 In the following sections the content of the curriculum is looked at from the point of view of five fairly broad aspects of the children's work with some assessment of the quality and range of work within each area.

ii LANGUAGE AND LITERACY

5.17 During the course of this survey objective tests in reading were administered to a sample of 11 year old children[1]. The results from these

---

[1] See Chapter 6 iii

tests are consistent with a rising trend in reading standards between 1955 and 1976–77[1]. This is supported by other findings from this survey which confirm that teachers gave a high degree of priority to the teaching of basic readings skills. The work children were given to do in reading was more closely matched to their capabilities for all ages and all levels of ability than work in any other area of the curriculum[2]. The ways in which 'match' was assessed are described in Chapter 6 ii and Annex B.

5.18 The primary school is particularly concerned with the development of language in the education of young children and every aspect of the children's work is influenced by the extent to which they use language with imagination, precision and accuracy. Much of the work undertaken in the primary school is designed with this in mind; through their work in all areas of the curriculum children extend and improve their ability to use language in a variety of contexts.

5.19 Competence in language develops through the interaction of listening, talking, reading, writing and children's own experience. Heads' comments indicate that this was widely recognised and the following statements of what they intended to achieve in the teaching of language in their schools are typical of many:

'To teach the basic skills of reading, spelling, handwriting, grammar, composition and comprehension.'

'To foster an enjoyment of poetry and literature and to get the children to think critically about what they read.'

'The aim is to teach children to enjoy their own language and literature and to enable them to express their own thoughts clearly, coherently and fluently.'

'To enable children to achieve a level of competence which will enable them to make their way when they leave the primary school.'

Listening and talking

5.20 Some witnesses to the Bullock Committee suggested that there had been a marked deterioration in children's ability to listen to their teachers

---

[1] See Appendix I
[2] See Annex to Chapter 6 Tables 30–32

reading or giving instructions[1]. The findings of this survey do not support this opinion. In over nine out of ten classes children were learning to follow instructions effectively, to understand the main ideas in information given to them and to follow the plot of a story ; in about four-fifths of the classes children also had the opportunity to listen to their teachers reading poetry.

5.21 There was some evidence, however, that these early listening skills were not being appropriately extended for some of the older children. Although four-fifths of the 11 year old classes were learning to comprehend the details in information they were given, in only about three-fifths of these classes were children learning to follow a sustained discussion and contribute appropriately and in fewer still were the children taught to follow the line of an argument.

5.22 A similar pattern emerged regarding the opportunities children had for talking. In almost all the classes children had the opportunity to talk informally among themselves at some time in the course of the working day. More formal arrangements for conversation which allowed controlled exchanges of ideas between children were increasingly common as the children grew older, being found in about half of 7 year old classes and approximately three-quarters of 11 year old classes. Typically children discussed stories, television or radio broadcasts, or cooperative work concerned with projects in history and geography, or worked out dramatic improvisations.

5.23 It is important that children have the opportunity to discuss with their teachers the work they are doing and the problems they may meet. This was given due place in about two-thirds of the 7 year old classes and almost half the 9 and 11 year old classes. It may well be that the more informal arrangements characteristic of the infant classes made it easier for this to happen. It was encouraging to find that in about four-fifths of all classes opportunities existed for children to talk with adults other than their own class teachers. Often this was with other teachers and sometimes with parents or other people who came to the school.

5.24 In nine-tenths of all the classes teachers ensured that children's vocabulary was steadily extended. This kind of work in language took place in all areas of the curriculum and was not limited to times devoted particularly to work in English. In about half the classes children were encouraged to elaborate and explain their answers or comments and were assisted, in this

---

[1] *A language for life'* Paragraph 10.19, HMSO

way, to find more precise and appropriate ways of describing what they had seen or experienced. However, in only about a fifth of the classes were children encouraged to formulate and pose pertinent questions or helped to find alternative ways of expressing themselves clearly and accurately.

5.25 Drama, whether considered as the dressing-up or role play of the younger children or the cooperative dramatising of a story or incident which occurred in the classes of older children, had a place in about half of the classes. In very few classes was drama exploited as a vehicle for the extension of children's spoken language.

Reading

5.26 As has already been noted (see paragraph 5.17) the teaching of the basic reading skills was accorded a high degree of priority. The use of graded reading schemes was universal in 7 year old classes and in nine out of ten of these classes children's reading practice was extended through the use of supplementary readers associated with these schemes. A very similar picture emerged in the 9 year old classes.

5.27 By the age of eleven, some children in three-quarters of the classes were making use of reading schemes and, in about four-fifths of the classes, of supplementary readers. In about a fifth of these older classes graded readers were given rather too much attention, at the expense of other more profitable forms of reading material. It was evident that teachers devoted considerable attention to ensuring that children mastered the basic techniques of reading but there was a tendency at all ages for children to receive insufficient encouragement to extend the range of their reading[1].

5.28 Children in about two-fifths of the 7 and 9 year old classes and in half the 11 year old classes appeared to turn readily and naturally to books for pleasure during the course of the day. In rather fewer classes the children appeared to use books with ease and confidence as a source of information. In almost all the classes there were some opportunities for children to select books for themselves. However, even by the age of eleven, this was given a high enough priority in only about two-fifths of the classes. Generally, more non-fiction than fiction was read by the children and poetry was read by children in about two-fifths of the 11 year old classes.

---

[1] See paragraph 5.47

5.29 In about a quarter of the 7 year old classes children's own speech and writing were used to provide early reading material for some children. Special arrangements for the withdrawal of individuals or groups of children for remedial help were made in half of the 9 and 11 year old classes and about two-fifths of the 7 year old classes[1].

5.30 For the abler readers, at all ages, there was little evidence that more advanced reading skills were being taught. The work which the ablest readers were given to do was too easy in about two-fifths of the classes[2]. Children were asked to comment on what they had read in about a third of the 7 year old classes, rising to three-fifths of 11 year old classes, but in only a very small minority of classes at any age were children discussing the books they had read at other than a superficial level of comprehension.

Writing

5.31 In just over half of the classes children did some writing on subjects of their own choice not connected directly with other current school work; such activities included describing events of interest, writing up information about things learned at home or at school, writing accounts for their diaries, retelling or making up stories, or describing favourite television programmes. In about two-fifths of 7 and 9 year old classes and in half of 11 year old classes the children did some writing which they initiated themselves and which arose from a range of studies currently being undertaken. In one class, for example, children were studying the trees near their school and each had chosen one of twelve related topics, suggested by the teacher, to follow up and write about. These topics included a detailed description of a chosen tree, observation of the form and foliage, an account of colonisation by plants and insects and the ways in which the timber could be used. Some children wrote pieces of imaginative prose and poetry about trees.

5.32 Children were frequently involved in writing tasks which had been set by teachers. These activities were more common than writing initiated by the children, and whether or not connected with other work in the curriculum, were found in three-quarters of 7 year old and four-fifths of 9 and 11 year old classes. The extent to which children were required to produce work set by teachers but not arising from other work or personal interests suggests that much less writing arose from pupils' own choice than is sometimes supposed.

[1] See Annex to Chapter 3, Table 17
[2] See Annex to Chapter 6, Table 32

5.33 In the Bullock Report is stated 'the experience of our visits was that much of the writing done in the name of topic work amounts to no more than copying'[1]. The evidence from the present survey also suggests this was happening quite extensively. There was copied writing from reference books in about two-thirds of 9 year old classes and in four out of five 11 year old classes; this was generally felt to be excessive. In four out of five classes children, on occasion, copied writing from the blackboard. The extent to which this was done was generally considered acceptable although it had too prominent a place in about a third of these classes.

5.34 Handwriting practice was provided in almost all the classes at all ages.

5.35 In virtually all the classes, children undertook some form of narrative writing, for example, relating stories, recounting adventure from real life or fantasy or describing their own experiences. The writing of prose or poetry which was expressive of feeling, often labelled 'creative writing', was not as strongly encouraged as might have been supposed. Where it fell into the category described in the Bullock Report as 'colourful or fanciful language, not "ordinary", using "vivid imagery" . . . very often divorced from real feeling'[2] then its absence can only be applauded. At its best personal writing enabled children to recreate experiences faithfully and sincerely and arose from the context of daily life in the classroom or outside. The amount of writing arising in this way increased with the age of the pupils, some examples being seen in about half of the 7 year old and in four out of five of the 11 year old classes.

5.36 It was rare to find children presented with a writing task which involved presenting a coherent argument, exploring alternative possibilities or drawing conclusions and making judgments. While it is recognised that this is a difficult form of writing for young children, it could have been more regularly encouraged among the older and abler pupils.

5.37 In just under half the classes children were actively encouraged to share with other pupils what they had written. For example, in some class-rooms children's stories had been collected together and placed in a book for other children to read. Stories and poems which had been written by the children were sometimes read aloud by the teacher or by the children. Some children were encouraged to write, act, tape or broadcast plays to the class or to the school, or to produce class or school magazines. Sometimes opportunities were found for children to write 'real' letters as,

[1] *A language for life*, p393, HMSO
[2] *A language for life*, p163, HMSO

for example, when a member of the class was in hospital, or as occasionally happened, the teacher arranged an exchange of correspondence with a class in another school.

5.38 Surprisingly, in only about a third of the classes were samples of children's written work regularly used to monitor their progress. In fewer than half of the classes was children's own written work used as a basis for teaching spelling, syntax, sentence structure or style.

Stimuli for language work

5.39 Children's own experiences frequently provided the basis for language work. Children were asked to talk and write about things which had happened to them out of school hours in about four-fifths of the classes. In a similar proportion of classes, school visits or school journeys provided the impetus for work in language.

5.40 The classroom, the school and its surroundings were extensively used to provide starting points for language activities. Approximately three-quarters of the 7 year old classes and nearly three-fifths of the older groups wrote and talked about animals, plants or things which were to be seen within the school, and nearly half the classes had produced work which was based on features of the school grounds or the immediate surroundings.

5.41 With the younger children particular emphasis was placed on imaginative and constructional play. Two-thirds of the 7 year old classes were encouraged through these kinds of activities to develop listening, speaking, reading and writing skills.

5.42 Teachers read or told stories in almost all 7 and 9 year old classes, and in nearly nine out of ten 11 year old classes. These stories, chosen from the wide repertoire of children's literature now available, ranged from traditional folk and fairy tales to modern stories of real life and fantasy. In particular, fiction based on historical periods and events, and science fiction, were popular with older juniors. Poetry was read to children in about nine out of ten classes in all three age groups. About a third of the classes were visited by speakers from outside the school.

5.43 Television programmes were introduced in more than four-fifths of classes and radio in about three-fifths of classes. Tape recordings were made by children in about a fifth of all the classes. Pre-recorded material was used in half of the classes.

5.44 Libraries and book collections were available almost universally, but in about three-fifths of the classes children had too little opportunity to use them for private reading of their own choice, or for reference. In three-quarters of the classes the books had been selected with care and represented a range of readng material containing, for example, interesting plots, good characterisation, clarity of illustration, factual accuracy and an index where appropriate, and suited to the age and reading abilities of the pupils.

5.45 Text books containing comprehension, grammar and language exercises were used to provide children with knowledge of language techniques and writing conventions, including spelling and syntax. Sometimes such material was introduced to support and develop children's individual written work, though the exercises chosen were not usually connected with pupils' own writing. Reliance on isolated exercises presented in text books does not necessarily provide children with the right kind of assistance in improving their capacity to use written language fluently and with purpose. Text books featured in the work of almost every 9 and 11 year old class, and of about two-thirds of 7 year old classes. Language course kits fulfil a similar function, but are generally presented as individual assignments that may be matched more closely to the reading abilities of the individual child. These kits were used in about half of the 9 and 11 year old classes and in a fifth of 7 year old classes. Other kinds of assignment cards were used for various purposes, from providing exercises in grammar or spelling, to stimulating creative writing. Whatever their particular intention, assignment cards usually provided starting points for individual work or occasionally for work in small groups, rather than for class work. These cards were introduced in about two-thirds of the classes.

Comment

5.46 On the evidence of this survey teachers in primary schools work hard to ensure that children master the basic techniques of reading and writing. There is little support for any view which considers that these aspects of language are neglected in primary schools. In the vast majority of classes reading schemes and courses were used to provide children with material at the right level of difficulty and were used regularly.

5.47 Graded reading schemes are of considerable value, particularly with the younger children. They provide a controlled rate of increase in the difficulty of words and phrases but in doing this certain limitations are imposed on the variety of the language used and the level of interest of the content. As soon as the children have gained some confidence in reading, these schemes should be supplemented with reading material which has been carefully selected to provide broader literary experience and extension of knowledge. Once the skills of decoding are firmly established further skills should be introduced. These include the efficient use of dictionaries and reference books, skimming passages for quick retrieval of information, scanning passages to establish the main points, the interpretation of context cues and the capacity to make sense of difficult passages. The teaching of these more advanced skills did not occur in three-quarters of 11 year old classes and even in the remaining quarter there was seldom planned and regular practice.

5.48 The learning and practice of skills, specific rules and conventions of English are all important parts of the acquisition of language competence, both written and spoken, and are more effectively taught when based on children's own language. The improvement of spoken language requires opportunities to engage in discussion and controlled intervention by the teacher.

5.49 Although all class teachers in the primary school are responsible for developing the use of children's language and must therefore be competent to teach reading and English language, it is probably not realistic to suppose that every teacher should acquire a high level of understanding and expertise in this as well as every other area of the curriculum. The Bullock Report's recommendation[1] that 'every school should have a suitably qualified teacher with responsibility for advising and supporting his colleagues in language and the teaching of reading' is probably the best way of ensuring that a high level of expertise is available in every school, but it is essential that the teacher concerned has the knowledge, the standing and the opportunity to carry out the duties implied by this role.

iii.   MATHEMATICS

5.50 The findings of this survey do not support the view which is sometimes expressed that primary schools neglect the practice of the basic skills in

[1] *A language for life*, Principal Recommendations 5, HMSO

arithmetic. In the classes inspected considerable attention was paid to computation, measurement and calculations involving sums of money, though the results of these efforts were disappointing in some respects.[1]

5.51 In describing what their schools set out to achieve in mathematics heads' comments indicated clearly that they attached considerable importance to children achieving competence in the basic skills of arithmetic and understanding mathematical processes. There was almost universal reference to the rules of addition, subtraction, multiplication and division, to computation and to concepts such as weight and number. This common view was reflected in the statement of one head who said his intentions were: 'To teach the children their tables. To teach the four rules of number in relation to money, decimals, fractions, time and measurement, along with some basic geometry. To show why and how these processes work so that children can understand them and use them accurately.' Many heads also referred to the importance of children gaining confidence, enjoyment and satisfaction from their work in mathematics.

5.52 Children were given individual assignments of work in mathematics in over four-fifths of all classes. In half of the 9 and 11 year old classes and in two-thirds of the 7 year old classes the allocation of individual assignments was a usual method adopted for organising the work in mathematics.[2] The presentation of assignments was usually by means of commercially published work cards, work cards devised by the teacher or, to a lesser extent, the use of text books.

5.53 In most classes where text books were used, they were employed appropriately to introduce a new aspect of mathematics or to provide suitable practice in a particular process. Commercial work cards were used to present work in almost all 9 and 11 year old classes and in nearly three-quarters of the 7 year old classes. Work cards devised by the teacher were less frequently used in the older classes but extensively used in 7 year old classes.

5.54 Children were grouped by ability for their work in mathematics more commonly than in any other subject.[3] There was a tendency in a number of classes to use individual work-card assignments when it would have been more appropriate to draw the group together to work from the blackboard or from a textbook. Direct teaching and discussion have an important part

---

[1] Chapter 6 iii; Appendix I
[2] See Annex to Chapter 3, Table 14
[3] See Annex to Chapter 3, Table 15

to play in the teaching of mathematics and in some classes this was inhibited by too great a reliance on the use of individual assignment cards. Television programmes were used in the teaching of mathematics in about a fifth of the 9 and 11 year old classes.

Content

5.55 In the majority of classes arithmetic was given appropriate attention and in no class was this aspect of the work in mathematics being ignored or neglected. In all the classes attention was given to calculations involving whole numbers and the processes of addition, subtraction, multiplication and division, although this kind of work was not sufficiently emphasised in about a fifth of the 7 year old classes. In about a third of the classes, at all ages, children were spending too much time undertaking somewhat repetitive practice of processes which they had already mastered. In these circumstances there was often a failure to make increasing demands on the children's speed or accuracy, or to introduce new and more demanding work. This and other issues concerning the teaching of mathematics are discussed in Chapter 6 iii and in Chapter 8 ii.

5.56 In almost all the classes some work was undertaken which was designed to help children to understand place value. Work was also given to help them to recognise simple number patterns. For the younger children this included activities such as counting by adding in 2s, 3s, 5s and 10s, doubling numbers or identifying odd and even numbers. For older children the work included the full range of multiplication tables and finding multiples and divisors beyond the limits of the tables. In nearly nine out of ten of the 11 year old classes this work involved drawing children's attention to some of the broader implications, such as understanding that the order of numbers can be changed without affecting the result in addition or multiplication but that this is not so in subtraction or division. This kind of work was taking place in less than half of the 7 year old classes.

5.57 Activities involving counting and estimating took place in most classes although there was room for more of this kind of work in about half of the classes. Practical activities designed to promote the understanding of quantitative description and the ideas of addition, subtraction, multiplication and division were introduced in well over four-fifths of the 9 and 11 year old classes and nearly all the 7 year old classes. However, in over half of these classes the practical activities undertaken were insufficiently demanding, for example, they were often confined to repetitive activities involving measuring and weighing and the children's attention was not drawn to the mathematical implications of what they were doing.

5.58 The notion of a fractional part was introduced when discussing every-day things in over half the 7 year old classes, four-fifths of 9 year old and nearly all 11 year old classes, although in many classes this was only touched on and the work was not fully developed. For the younger children the work was mainly concerned with practical activities involving halves, quarters or thirds, while the older children progressed to the idea of equivalence and the techniques employed in the calculation of fractions. In a few 7 year old classes children were introduced to the notion of decimals, usually associated with the recording of amounts of money or metric measures. It was more common for such teaching to be introduced at a later stage, within the programme of about three-quarters of 9 year old classes and almost all 11 year old classes. Nine out of ten 11 year old classes were taught to carry out calculations involving the four rules of number to two decimal places or more.

5.59 The importance of learning to handle money in everyday transactions and acquiring a sense of its value in relation to simple purchases was recognised in almost all the classes. Work involving the measurement of length, weight, area and time took place at some time in nine out of ten classes at all ages, the work progressing as the children grew older. For example, while 7 year olds were frequently taught to tell the time or measure each other's height, 11 year olds were often introduced to the twenty-four hour clock, carrying out assignments based on rail or flight schedules, or to activities such as calculating the area of the playground or the height of the school building. Occasionally such work was linked to ideas in elementary physics as, for example, when the children in an 11 year old class made simple pendulums, recorded the number and rate of oscillations and deter-mined their relationship to the length of string and the weight of the pendulum bob. In another 11 year old class the study of a river in science involved the estimation and calculation of speeds and the amount of water flowing; the children measured the width and depth of the river and the slope and angles of the bank.

5.60 When children are asked to 'find the answer' to a problem in arithmetic, they are usually being asked to complete an unfinished state-ment; for example, 'six and nine more make ......', or '$81 - 16 = ...$', or again '$(4 \times 320) - (2 \times 55) = ...$'. If, however, the missing part lies in the middle of the statement it may be represented by a symbol; for example $6 + \square = 15$, or again $1280 - \square = 1170$. The use of symbols gives precision in the recording of mathematical statements; some symbols are essential to any progress in mathematics and were taught in all classes. In about half of the classes children were introduced to additional symbols such as 'box' diagrams or arrows. Where children understood the meaning of these symbols, and could use them appropriately to express a mathematical relationship, this provided a useful dimension to their work in mathematics. For some children, however, a proliferation of symbols tended to create confusion rather than clarification. In some cases, particularly in the older classes, more attention could usefully have been given to more precise and unambiguous use of ordinary language to describe the properties of number, size, shape or position.

5.61 Children used various forms of visual presentation for their work in mathematics in about four-fifths of all the classes. This ranged from making simple table squares with multiples picked out in colour, to the drawing or construction of block or line graphs, pie-charts or three-dimensional shapes. In about a fifth of the classes there was evidence of mathematics being linked to work in other areas of the curriculum, and this sometimes provided opportunities for visual presentation of mathematical data. For example in an 11 year old class children visited a church as part of a local study and were able to watch the bellringers at work. They observed the different order of the changes rung and, on their return to school, considered the possible permutations. Subsequently the children devised a diagram to illustrate the possible sequences.

5.62 Mention has already been made of the link between mathematics and physical science. This connection could be more fully exploited in the work children do both in mathematics and science as in a 9 year old class where children were constructing a model following a visit to a windmill; discussion of the gears provided the teacher with the opportunity to introduce the notion of ratio and to follow this up in the children's work in mathematics. Again, in a 7 year old class the children were working on 'ourselves' as a mathematical topic. They recorded and constructed graphs of their bodily measurements and, using a stopwatch, recorded each other's variations of pulse rate following the performance of a number of different physical activities.

5.63 Many ideas encountered by children, for example weight, volume, density, speed or velocity are common to mathematics and physical science but the connection was rarely made explicit. Similarly, precise measurement is essential to both disciplines but techniques of measurement acquired in mathematics were seldom applied to the children's work in experimental science or vice versa. Geography is another subject where ideas common to both subjects, for example, scale, coordinates, direction finding, angles, or longitude and latitude, were seldom linked in the work which children did in either subject; much more could be done in this way, especially with the older children.

Comment

5.64 Mathematics is given a high degree of priority in the curriculum of the primary school. For average and less able children within the classes inspected the work in mathematics, together with that in reading, was more consistently matched to children's capabilities than their work in any other area of the curriculum.[1] However, for the children who showed most marked mathematical ability the work was often too easy and it is a matter for concern that these children's abilities were not fully extended in their work in this subject.[2] The responses to the NFER mathematics test E2 show that the efforts made to teach children to calculate are not rewarded by high scores in the examples concerned with the handling of everyday situations. Learning to operate with numbers may need to be more closely linked with learning to use them in a variety of situations than is now common.

5.65 The extensive use of individual work-card assignments resulted in some children repeating known processes rather than being taken on to the next stage of their learning. In addition there is a place for more direct teaching of a whole group or class in mathematics. Most classes were grouped according to their attainments for work in mathematics and this arrangement could provide opportunities for teachers to deal with a particular topic or process with a whole group. In some cases it is more efficient to teach the whole class than to attempt to teach each new aspect of mathematics individually to each child. Challenging questions and quick recall of number facts, including multiplication tables, are essential in the learning of mathematics and often require a lively and sustained contact between a teacher and a group of children.

---

[1] See Chapter 6 ii and Annex to Chapter 6, Tables 30–32.
[2] See Annex to Chapter 6, Table 32.

iv. SCIENCE

5.66 Few primary schools visited in the course of this survey had effective programmes for the teaching of science. There was a lack of appropriate equipment; insufficient attention was given to ensuring proper coverage of key scientific notions; the teaching of processes and skills such as observing, the formulating of hypotheses, experimenting and recording was often superficial. The work in observational and experimental science was less well matched to children's capabilities than work in any other area of the curriculum.[1]

5.67 Heads' statements showed that the degree to which programmes of work in science had been thought out varied considerably from school to school. A number of heads referred to the importance of developing children's powers of observation, and to the responsibility of schools to encourage enquiry and curiosity. One wrote that his intention was 'to encourage in the children an attitude of wonder and enquiry so that these may become a lasting part of their life and outlook and to assist children's desire to communicate and construct; and help them to gain an insight into the happenings of everyday life'.

5.68 Some heads also mentioned the scientific subject matter they considered children should study; for example, 'practical work in nature study, plant and animal life, and an introduction to a study of the environment'. Another head wrote: 'The children should be able to perceive relationships and pose hypotheses to be tested through experiments, to be discarded if found untenable; they should become acquainted with the evolution and metamorphosis of animals; learn the simple properties of air and water; and understand how simple machines work'.

5.69 Science is a way of understanding the physical and biological world. However, the general impression given by heads' statements was that only a small minority recognised the important contribution which science could make to children's intellectual development. Although some science was attempted in a majority of classes, the work was developed seriously in only just over one class in ten, either as a study in its own right, or in relation to other topics being studied. The attention given to science did not vary greatly with the age of the children.

5.70 In science it is essential that children should develop observational skills and begin to recognise similarities and differences. The study of

---

[1] See Chapter 6 ii and Annex to Chapter 6, Tables 30–32.

living and non-living things can stimulate children to ask the sort of questions which can lead, with careful guidance, to the formulation of hypotheses and the devising of experiments to test them.

5.71 In about two-thirds of all the classes a nature table or 'interest' table was kept, where objects such as pieces of wood, sea shells, building materials, old clocks or radios were collected and displayed. In a similar number of classes plants were either grown in school or brought in for study. About half the classes kept small mammals such as hamsters or gerbils and a similar proportion undertook some work arising from outdoor activities such as a nature walk, a visit to a local park or the study of a local habitat such as a canal or pond.

5.72 Unfortunately, although children in a fair proportion of the classes were introduced to plants, animals and objects intended to stimulate scientific enquiry, in very few classes were opportunities taken to teach children how to make careful observations or to plan and carry out investigations of a scientific nature. For example, collections of autumn leaves were commonly used for decorative purposes or to stimulate work with pattern and colour; they were seldom used to help children to recognise similarities and differences in formation, such as the different forms of multiple leaf in ash and horse-chestnut trees, or notions of stability and change in living things.

5.73 In about two-fifths of the classes some use was made of television broadcasts for the teaching of science, but radio was used in less than one class in ten. In some classes a particular television or radio broadcast was selected to fit in with a topic the class was studying, and in others part of a term's work was planned around a series of programmes. Used in these ways, television and radio broadcasting made a valuable contribution to the work in science and it is surprising that, in a subject where many teachers lacked confidence in their own abilities, more use was not made of this resource to support the work in science.

5.74 Text-books or assignment cards were used to initiate work in science in only about a fifth of all the classes, although their use increased with the age of the children. At the 11 year old level about a quarter of the classes made use of assignment cards and a similar proportion worked with text-books. The discriminating use of carefully chosen text-books or assignment cards can help to sustain work in science if their use is carefully planned to supplement a programme of work; more use of this resource to support a particular line of scientific enquiry could have been made. Considerable use was made of reference books in nearly two-thirds of the 7 year old classes and four out of five of the 11 year old classes. However, in only about a fifth of the classes were reference books well used to support first hand observation or experimental work or to develop sustained work on a particular topic.

5.75 Children's interests arising from their life at home, outside school or on holiday sometimes provide starting points for work in science. There was some evidence in about two-fifths of the classes that work had arisen in this way, although the potential of such work was seldom exploited. Children may collect shells, pebbles or fir cones; may wonder why aeroplanes stay in the air or how a canal lock works; may become interested in the behaviour and characteristics of animals or immersed in the details of the latest space exploration reported on television. There is a wealth of experience for teachers to draw on, and most children are willing to bring things to school and discuss their enthusiasm in class.

5.76 Although four-fifths of all classes had access to some resources for their work in science, the provision was generally inadequate. Simple equipment for measuring, observing and discriminating, for example, thermometers, hand lenses, tuning forks, and materials such as batteries, bulbs and wire for work with electricity, can be assembled easily but were rarely seen to be available in the classroom. Older children were only marginally better catered for than the younger children in this respect.

Content

5.77 In interpreting the findings relating to the content and quality of children's work in science it has to be kept in mind that there was no evidence of such work in nearly a fifth of all the classes. In those classes where work in science was undertaken, about half had touched on topics which contributed to children's understanding of the characteristics of living things and to notions of stability and change in living organisms. Fewer classes gave attention to reproduction, growth and development in plants and animals. Sources of energy were considered in about half of the 11 year old classes but rarely by the younger children.

5.78 In only half the 11 year old classes and about a third of the 7 and 9 year old classes were children prompted to look for and identify significant patterns, for example, the way leaves are arranged on a twig, patterns of bird migration, the way materials react to heat or light, or the arrangement of colours in a rainbow, and the way light behaves when it is reflected, casts shadows or is dispersed into its component parts. Such topics can be developed without specialised facilities, using simple materials such as twigs, water, salt or mirrors or simply carrying out observations in a natural habitat. In only a very small minority of classes were activities requiring careful observation and accurate recording developed beyond a superficial level and in less than one class in thirty was there evidence of investigations which had been initiated as a result of questions asked by the children.

5.79 In those classes where efforts were made to introduce children to science as both a body of organised knowledge and an experimental process the emphasis tended to be placed on work relating to plants and animals. This probably reflects the fact that rather more teachers were knowledgeable in the field of biology than in the physical sciences, although some were able to extend the work to take account of physical as well as biological aspects. For example, in one 9 year old class the teacher had arranged a visit to a bird sanctuary. The preparatory work involved drawing children's attention to the characteristics of different species of birds which would assist in their identification, examining the construction of birds' nests and relating the materials used and the method of construction to the size of the bird and the shape of the beak. At a later stage the children constructed a bird table and went on to collect bird droppings; they placed them in sterilised seed compost and witnessed the germination of seeds which had been carried by the birds. In an 11 year old class where germination was being studied, the children were growing plants under different conditions and recording their findings in a systematic way. They were being encouraged to make predictions and generalise from their findings; the teacher was also able to introduce the notion of the need for a control sample.

5.80 Another school had its own small area of woodland in part of a nearby Forestry Commission plantation. The children in the 11 year old class had planted seedlings and were carrying out systematic observations of their growth. They also made careful comparisons of other plants and animals found on open ground, on the fringes, and in the centre of the woodland. This included the observation and identification of living things found under stones and logs and on the trees. In the course of these activities the children designed and constructed clinometers and other instruments to enable them to measure dimensions such as the height and girth of the trees and the spread of the branches. The children had learned to distinguish hard and soft timber and had employed a rigorous technique for comparing the hardness of woods by dropping a weight from a standard height on to a nail in the wood. The children were knowledgeable about the kinds of wood appropriate to different forms of manufacturing, for example, paper and matchsticks, and the types used in the construction of different household articles.

5.81 Studies relating specifically to man-made artefacts or mechanical actions were comparatively rare, although one 9 year old class had paid a visit to a working water mill. During the visit the children made notes and drawings and, on their return to school, were able to construct a working model to illustrate the action they had observed at the mill. Subsequently the children looked at other applications of the mechanics of a chain of cogwheels including the gears of a bicycle, the action of an alarm clock and a rotary food whisk. The study of mechanical artefacts supported by constructional activities is an aspect of the work in science which is seldom exploited and which could usefully be developed at the primary stage.

Comment

5.82 During the past few years considerable efforts have been made to stimulate and support science teaching in primary schools. There have been curriculum development projects at national level and in some areas local authority advisers and teachers' centres have been very active. Guidance about the kind of science which is suitable for young children, its place in the curriculum and teaching methods is readily available in the publications of the Schools Council, the Nuffield Foundation, the Department of Education and Science and elsewhere. Yet the progress of science teaching in primary schools has been disappointing ; the ideas and materials produced by curriculum development projects have had little impact in the majority of schools.

5.83 The most severe obstacle to the improvement of science in the primary school is that many existing teachers lack a working knowledge of elementary science appropriate to children of this age. This results in some teachers being so short of confidence in their own abilities that they make no attempt to include science in the curriculum. In other cases, teachers make this attempt but the work which results is superficial since the teachers themselves may be unsure about where a particular investigation or topic in science could lead.

5.84 Making good the lack of science expertise among existing teachers is a complex matter but the careful deployment of those teachers who do have a background of study in science is a straightforward step that should be taken. Such teachers should be encouraged to use their expertise to the full, as class and specialist teachers, to bring about an improvement in the standards children achieve in science. Teachers with a particular responsibility for science need to be supported fully by heads and advisers and where necessary receive further in-service training, particularly courses which are designed to help them to further their own knowledge of science. The planned acquisition and use of resources for science teaching would also contribute to a general improvement of the work in this area. In addition, more attention should be given to the ways in which initial training courses can best equip new teachers to undertake the teaching of science whether as a class teacher, as a science consultant, or as a specialist in the primary school.

v. AESTHETIC AND PHYSICAL EDUCATION

5.85 Aesthetic education may arise in connection with work in any area of the curriculum. This section is concerned with those subjects which contribute particularly to the development of children's aesthetic response through making and doing, looking and listening, and touching and moving.

Art and crafts

5.86 Some form of art and craft activity was undertaken by every class. In almost every classroom, and often in the corridors, halls and other shared spaces there were displays of children's work. In their comments a number of heads emphasised the importance of the visual environment created within the school and its effect on the children.

5.87 It was common practice for teachers to initiate work in art and craft by directing children's attention to arrangements and displays both inside and outside the classroom, and, to a lesser extent to the immediate environment of the school. Displays of natural objects such as plants, rocks or shells were introduced as a stimulus for work in over three-quarters of the classes although there was seldom sufficiently careful observation and discussion before the work was begun. Drawing or modelling from direct observation was rarely encouraged, although there was some interesting work which arose in this way. For example, in one 9 year old class the children made very careful and thorough observations of stick insects feeding on privet leaves. Using hand lenses to assist their observation of the details they made charcoal or pencil drawings of various parts of the insects before beginning work on their pictures.

5.88 In another 9 year old class a collection of Anglo-Saxon pottery had been borrowed from a local museum and children were able to handle and examine the pottery before making their own clay pots. Man-made objects were less frequently used than natural objects as starting points for work in art and crafts, and the observation of mechanical artefacts was rare. It was encouraging to see assignments of the sort undertaken in one 11 year old class where bicycles had been brought into the school playground and the children studied and drew the various parts with considerable care. The drawings were intended to record differences in the style of construction and to demonstrate how the working parts operated.

5.89 While almost every class had some materials for drawing, painting and print-making, materials for modelling and three-dimensional construction were available in under two-thirds of the classes. The quality of materials was reasonably satisfactory in over half of the classes but there were indications that more discrimination in the selection of materials by teachers and more care in the subsequent storage of materials and equipment would have contributed to better standards of work in some classes.

5.90 The use of pattern and colour was generally given more attention than form and texture in the work that children did. Children in four out of five classes were taught to handle tools, equipment and materials carefully and safely. Although children in the majority of classes were being taught to choose materials with some discrimination, satisfactory standards in the execution of the work were achieved in only about a third of the classes. Often the unsatisfactory standards resulted from insufficient guidance in the use of appropriate techniques.

5.91 About a third of the classes visited local art galleries, exhibitions or museums and it was encouraging to note that about one class in ten was visited by local craftsmen or artists.

5.92 Drawing, painting and modelling were frequently employed to record observations and information in other areas of the curriculum. Four-fifths of the 11 year old classes used these techniques to illustrate their work in geography and history; among the younger children this kind of activity was more often associated with the illustration of stories and poems. Large murals, either painted or constructed with collage assembled from scrap material, were often used to depict a scene, for example from *The Pied Piper of Hamelin* or an underwater scene from *The Water Babies*. There is a place for this kind of large scale construction of a picture, which has the advantage that several children, or even a whole class, can contribute to a joint enterprise, but care needs to be taken to ensure that sufficient demands are made on individual children and that the work does not become purely mechanical and repetitive.

5.93 Drawing and modelling techniques were employed in mathematics in about two-thirds of the classes, for example, in the telling presentation of block graphs, the delineation of patterns or the accurate construction of three-dimensional shapes. Drawings and coloured line illustrations were used to record work in geography, history, religious education and science. Three-dimensional construction was most often associated with geography and history; the link between constructional work and the study of artefacts and mechanical actions in science was seldom exploited.

5.94 While almost all the classes undertook some practical work in art and some crafts, there is a need for children to be taught to observe more carefully and to record faithfully what they see and know. The emphasis which has been placed on children using a wide variety of materials has in some cases resulted in children working in a superficial way. Children need time to familiarise themselves with the characteristics of particular materials and to acquire some degree of mastery over essential skills and techniques. A more carefully selected range of art and craft activities, worked at more thoroughly, would enable children to reach higher standards in the execution of their work and obtain more satisfaction from it.

5.95 In about a tenth of 9 and 11 year old classes boys and girls were separated for craft activities. On these occasions girls often undertook needlecraft while boys did some form of constructional work. The comparative neglect of three-dimensional construction is disappointing; opportunities should be provided for the older children, both boys and girls, to undertake some work with wood and other resistant materials and to learn to handle the tools and techniques associated with them. The standard of two and three-dimensional work in 7 year old classes was generally more satisfactory than in the older classes and was consistently better matched to the children's abilities.[1]

---

[1] See Annex to Chapter 6, Tables 30–32,

Music

5.96 In music, as with art and crafts, children in every class in the survey had some experience of this subject. Heads' comments about what their schools set out to achieve in music were generally practical and precise. The following is typical of many comments: 'Children should have experience of sound and rhythm in music through listening and through participation. They should have the opportunity to experience music through movement, singing and the use of tuned and untuned percussion instruments'. Another head wrote: 'Children should have the opportunity to take part in music-making and have the experience of playing an instrument. Opportunities should be provided for children to listen to and enjoy a range of good music'.

5.97 The teaching of music was supported in a variety of ways to ensure that all the classes received some teaching in this subject. Music was the subject most frequently taught by a teacher other than the class teacher and, in 11 year old classes, the subject for which peripatetic teachers were most often employed.[1] In addition, particular responsibility for music was allocated more frequently than for any other subject.[2] Peripatetic teachers generally undertook the teaching of stringed instruments, and occasionally brass and woodwind, to individuals or small groups of children. Some peripatetic music teachers worked with the whole class but this was less common.

5.98 Radio programmes in particular were used for music teaching in three-fifths of the classes and made a significant contribution to the music curriculum. In part this is a tribute to well established programmes which have won the confidence of many teachers. It was noticeable that the introduction of songs and simple accompaniments during the course of these programmes was frequently followed up by teachers who made no claim to musicianship but felt it important that their classes should have the opportunity for this kind of work. Also most schools now have equipment providing a reasonable quality of sound reproduction and recorded music was introduced to children in four-fifths of the classes.

5.99 The use of tuned and untuned percussion instruments provided a simple and enjoyable introduction to music-making for many children. They were used for accompaniment in nearly all 7 year old classes and in four-

---

[1] See Annex to Chapter 3, Tables 19 and 20.
[2] See Annex to Chapter 4, Table 24.

fifths of the 9 and 11 year old classes. Improvisation or 'creative' music-making was encouraged in half of the classes. In some cases children composed their own tunes or sound pictures and made their own arrangements with instruments such as recorders, glockenspiels, chime bars, xylophones, triangles, drums and cymbals. The reading of musical notation was introduced in nearly two-fifths of 7 year old classes, two-thirds of 9 year old and three-quarters of 11 year old classes.

5.100 The quality of the musical experience provided for children varied, not surprisingly, according to the talents and expertise of the teachers and the availability of peripatetic teaching in different areas of the country. There were some schools where heads and teachers, over a period of time, had built up a strong tradition of music-making involving choirs, orchestras and instrumental groups. Individual teachers who were able to play instruments were often willing to play alongside children and to teach groups of children who were interested to learn, sometimes on a voluntary basis in the lunch hour or after school.

5.101 Music played an important part in the school assembly. In some cases children were able to accompany hymns and songs with recorders, percussion instruments, guitars and occasionally the violin or piano. The school assembly also provided an opportunity for the introduction of recorded music and some schools made a feature of this, introducing a different composer or theme each week.

5.102 Movement with music was undertaken in four-fifths of the 7 year old classes and about half of the older classes. School plays or other special performances often involved music; one school was engaged in a production of *The Owl and the Pussycat* with music specially written by the peripatetic music teacher who taught general class music and the guitar. In the relatively few classes where French was taught, songs were used to extend children's vocabulary and to introduce variety and enjoyment.

5.103 Singing was taught in all the classes and the quality of the songs chosen was generally good. Particularly for the younger children, well chosen songs often provided an important extension of their experience of language. In learning to read children require the ability to make quite fine aural discriminations between different sounds; rhymes, singing games and well chosen songs can often assist in this process and generally encourage aural awareness.

5.104 The special provision made for the teaching of music ensured that children in all the classes had some experience of work in music. While the quality of work varied greatly among schools according to the level of musicianship available, the services of specialist and peripatetic teachers made a valuable contribution to the music education received by children. This support was generally directed towards those children who showed some ability in music and for whom instrumental teaching was provided. In the general class work, levels of achievement were considerably more modest and although children generally appeared to enjoy their music-making, the quality of the work inevitably reflected the teacher's competence as a musician.

Physical education

5.105 Every class in the survey undertook some form of physical activity, although the emphasis given to games, gymnastics, dance or swimming differed according to the facilities and opportunities available in a particular school and according to the age of the children. It was not usual for boys and girls to be separated for their work in physical education; such separation occurred in only just over one in twenty 9 and 11 year old classes. One head, typical of many, commented that in his school the intention in physical education was to encourage 'experience of body movement through dance, drama and large physical movements such as climbing, balancing and swimming'.

5.106 Gymnastics was included in the curriculum of well over four-fifths of all the classes. Opportunities for swimming increased with the age of the children: only a quarter of 7 year old classes were taught swimming compared with two-thirds of 9 year old and nine out of ten 11 year old classes.

5.107 Some form of equipment for gymnastics was available to about nine out of ten classes, while games equipment and other small apparatus was used by almost every class. The high incidence of swimming for the 11 year old classes reflects local education authority policies. Where a pool was not available on the school premises, most authorities arranged for children to make use of the local baths. Where necessary, transport was provided and swimming instruction given at the baths. In many areas it was only possible to provide this facility for the older pupils, although occasionally younger children were able to take advantage of such provision, particularly in the summer term.

5.108 Comment on the quality of the work in physical education has to be treated with caution since, quite reasonably, in about a quarter of the classes not all the relevant activities took place during the period of the inspection. No attempt was made to assess the quality of the swimming instruction for the purposes of this survey because of the time that would have been required for visits away from the school premises.

5.109 In 9 and 11 year old classes team games were played in almost all the classes, often with considerable enthusiasm on the children's part. Not surprisingly, this was the aspect of physical education in which these older children achieved the greatest degree of skill. In dance, even in the 7 year old classes where this activity was most often encouraged, sensitivity in the use of movement was seldom achieved. About three-fifths of the 7 year old classes used radio programmes to supplement the work in movement and where these were followed up with appropriate practice and extension of the ideas presented, they made a useful contribution to their work. There were also opportunities to link the experience of music and movement to work in language and art.

5.110 The work in gymnastics was very uneven in quality. This was undoubtedly in part due to considerable discrepancies in the nature of the facilities available. In some schools, particularly those with few children on roll, often in rural areas, no hall was available for gymnastics and this made it necessary either to clear classrooms of furniture or to work outside whenever the weather was suitable. In almost all schools that had a hall it was necessary to use it for a variety of purposes, including assemblies, music and drama and, in some cases, the midday meal.

5.111 The type of work undertaken in gymnastics also varied. Some schools continued to pursue a programme of traditional educational gymnastics with the emphasis on sensitivity and the ability to invent sustained sequences of movement, while others had clearly been strongly influenced by the British Amateur Gymnastic Association's award scheme. Some teachers were qualified coaches and others had been influenced by the coaching schemes. A number of schools organised voluntary clubs, particularly in association with the BAGA scheme, which were enthusiastically supported by the children. When expert coaching of this sort was available this was often reflected in the quality of the general class work, where children showed increasing versatility and confidence in their own physical abilities.

5.112 The stage at which children were introduced to major team games such as football and netball varied according to the circumstances of the school. Many schools were able to make use of local parks or sports centres for the older children. In the 7 year old classes children mainly worked in small groups practising various skills such as throwing, catching or kicking. Older children were generally eager to take part in team games and in many schools there were teachers who voluntarily devoted much extra time to organising inter-school matches and practice sessions.

5.113 In 11 year old classes, next to music, physical education was the subject most frequently taught by a teacher other than the normal class teacher.[1] This would seem to be reflected in the quality of the teaching as, after reading and mathematics, the work in physical education was most frequently suitably matched to the children's abilities at all ages.[2]

5.114 All children were offered the opportunity to participate in some form of physical education, although schools placed different emphasis on the relative importance of individual sporting activities, team games, gymnastics, dance or swimming. The type of facilities available and the interests and skills of individual teachers undoubtedly played a large part in influencing the balance of the programme in physical education. As a consequence, the extent and quality of work differed considerably from school to school; however it is evident that most schools thought it important to provide as good a range of physical activities as was possible with the resources and facilities available.

vi. SOCIAL STUDIES

5.115 Many primary schools used a thematic approach to the work in social studies and a wide variety of topics were introduced at each age level. Often the environment of the school, or a place within easy reach of it, was the focus of this kind of work, although children also studied other countries and other times. In the course of these studies material was most often drawn from historical and geographical sources, although some schools also, on occasion, chose topics with a religious dimension.

Religious education

5.116 The place of religious education in schools is supported by the

---

[1] See Annex to Chapter 3 Table 20.
[2] See Annex to Chapter 3, Tables 30–32.

statutory requirements of the 1944 Education Act and, for all county and voluntary controlled schools, by agreed syllabuses which have been produced or adopted by the local education authorities. Almost three-quarters of all schools — county, voluntary and aided — made an explicit reference to using an agreed syllabus.

5.117 Nearly a quarter of all heads referred specifically to Christian teaching. Other heads, not exclusively from denominational schools, emphasized equally strongly the particular Christian commitment of their schools. Both heads' written comments and the work in the classes indicated that Christian precepts were seen as important ideas to be taught and put into practice.

5.118 Teaching of this kind was often associated with work on a general topic such as 'helping other people' which could be related to the children's everyday experience or to geographical or historical contexts. Religious themes associated with work in history and geography were introduced in about a fifth of the 7 year old classes and almost two-thirds of the older classes. A few schools had also introduced work on other faiths which often included reference to other countries and to the historical origins of these faiths.

5.119 In four-fifths of the classes children were learning about man's attempt to frame religious and moral values and the Bible was the most common source of material used. For example, in some classes both the New and Old Testaments were being used to illuminate or provoke consideration of ideas such as forgiveness or to give instruction in specifically religious ideas or practices, including those associated with the church calendar. Sometimes the Bible was used to provide a story from which children might gain some understanding of man's spiritual dilemmas.

Assemblies

5.120 In nearly all the assemblies taking place in schools there was a religious content. Various forms of assembly took place, often within the same school. Some were led by the head or another teacher and some were taken by the children. There were the simple occasions consisting of a hymn and a prayer, perhaps with some comment from the head or with readings from the Bible or other religious literature. Some assemblies were based on a theme such as 'honesty', or on a story such as 'the good Samaritan'.

5.121 Assemblies presented by the children involved careful preparation and often fostered a sense of community and participation. Drama was associated with religious education in about a third of the classes and the dramatisation of a bible story or other kind of story was often introduced into the assembly. Music was an important feature of most assemblies and children were sometimes able to accompany the hymn singing with a variety of instruments including recorders and percussion instruments.

5.122 The survey was not designed to provide a close study of religious education in schools but the evidence indicates that primary schools were generally concerned to provide children with a religious education based on the Bible and on Christian beliefs and values. However, in practice it does appear that in many schools the curriculum in religious education was somewhat restricted. Consideration might usefully be given to ways in which the range of work in the subject could be expanded to respond more fully to the challenge of living in a multi-faith society.

History

5.123 Some attention was given to the study of the past in three-fifths of the 7 year old classes, nine out of ten 9 year old classes and almost all 11 year old classes. Often the work was part of a general topic such as 'ships' or related to a current event. For example, the preparations for the Queen's Silver Jubilee prompted a number of classes to look back to the events of coronation year and in some cases to compare the present times with those of Elizabeth I. In the younger classes historical reference tended to be rather incidental, although by the age of eleven the work was more recognisably historical. Some classes were studying periods of English history, often with a bias towards work on buildings and costumes. This kind of work was frequently stimulated by a visit to a nearby castle or other building or a site of historical significance.

5.124 Collections of artefacts and documents were occasionally used, often being provided by a local museum. This practice tended to increase with the age of the children. The 11 year old classes more often drew on accounts of past events which people known to the children could recall, although this source was also occasionally used by younger children. In one 11 year old class grandparents had been invited to the school to talk about their experience of unemployment in the 1930s and the children were able to draw comparisons with the present day, particularly since their school was situated in an area of high unemployment.

5.125 Television programmes provided the basis for work in history in about a quarter of the 7 year old classes and two-fifths of the 11 year old classes. For most children the programmes were a useful source of information and occasionally they formed an integral part of a well planned scheme of work with careful preparation before viewing and thorough follow-up afterwards.

5.126 Most 9 and 11 year old classes used history reference books, the quality of which was reasonably good in about three-quarters of the classes. The history reference books in 7 year old classes were less likely to be satisfactory. Stories with a historical setting were used to initiate work in about half the 9 year old classes and two-thirds of the 11 year old classes. History text books and published work cards were used in three-fifths of the 9 and 11 year old classes but only rarely in the 7 year old classes.

5.127 Taken as a whole in four out of five of all the classes which studied history the work was superficial. In many cases it involved little more than copying from reference books and often the themes chosen had very little historical content. In some classes children moved from one assignment to another in a fairly random way so that work on Ancient Greece might immediately precede or even follow a study of 'travel in Stuart times'. It was rare to find classes where the work, even in a simple way, was leading the children towards an understanding of historical change and the causal factors involved, or where children were becoming aware of the nature of historical evidence.

5.128 A factor contributing to this situation was undoubtedly a lack of planning in the work. Few schools had schemes of work in history, or teachers who were responsible for the planning and implementation of work in this field.[1] While it is true that an appreciation of the perspective of time develops only slowly in children, it is liable to remain rudimentary unless a coherent approach to helping children acquire an understanding of the past is adopted. Where history was taught through topics of general interest there was the danger of a fragmented approach. A framework is required to provide some ordering of the content being taught. This may be a single path through a chronological sequence or a more complex series of historical topics which, while not necessarily taught in chronological order, should give a perspective in terms of the ordering of events or by means of comparison with the present day.

---

[1] See Annex to Chapter 4, Tables 24 and 25.

Geography

5.129 Some work of a geographical nature was undertaken in three-fifths of the 7 year old classes and nine out of ten 9 and 11 year old classes. The 7 year olds learned about the immediate environment and more distant places to the same extent. Similar topics, for example, 'homes', or 'life on the farm' or 'children of other lands' tended to appear in classes of all ages. This practice can lead to unnecessary repetition unless considerable care is taken to ensure there is progression in the work which children do.

5.130 Two-fifths of the 7 year old classes and two-thirds of the 11 year old classes carried out geographical studies in the local environment. Some work relating to local population, agriculture, industry, transport, land features or resources took place in nearly half of the older classes although work relating to other countries was also more common in these classes.

5.131 Some of the most successful work was based on the locality of the school, as in a 9 year old class where a proposed new road to by-pass the town stimulated work which involved consideration of the local amenities and transport links. The children studied local maps and illustrations and carried out a traffic and pedestrian survey as well as considering alternative routes for the proposed new road.

5.132 Local features such as a woodland or river were sometimes used to stimulate consideration of land formation. More use could have been made of work based on local industries, as in an 11 year old class which visited a local timber yard and subsequently traced the origins of the timber, both imported and local, and the destinations and use of the products.

5.133 Reference books were frequently used for work in geography and about three-fifths of the 11 year old classes made use of textbooks and work-cards. Atlases were used in about three-quarters of the 11 year old classes but globes were introduced in only three-fifths of these classes and much less frequently in the younger classes. Maps of the locality were used in only about a quarter of the 9 year old classes and in about two-fifths of the 11 year old classes.

5.134 Television was used to introduce or reinforce work in about a quarter of the classes and usually made a positive contribution to the children's understanding of some of the geographical influences on people's lives. Radio was used to a lesser extent but made an equally useful contribution when it was.

5.135 To a limited extent children were being helped to acquire an appreciation of man's dependence on natural phenomena and resources in a quarter of the 7 year old classes and in about three-fifths of the older classes. However, as with history, much of the work tended to be superficial and there was often little evidence of progression. For example the observation and recording of weather conditions which was common in 7 year old classes rarely developed into a more wide ranging study of climate for the older pupils.

5.136 There were substantial numbers of classes where no use was made of atlases, maps or globes. Even where work centred on the neighbourhood of the school, maps of the locality were introduced relatively infrequently. Though good work was being done in some classes, in the majority essential skills and ideas were seldom given sufficient attention; work in geography cannot be soundly based if children are not introduced to the essential skills of the subject.

6 The curriculum: scope and standards of work

i. SUITABILITY OF RANGE

6.1 In making general statements about the quality of the work of primary schools it is as important to consider the range of the curriculum studied as to make judgements about standards in particular parts of it. The evidence of the survey confirms what is largely common knowledge, namely that the range of work and the standards achieved are interrelated, sometimes in ways that are not immediately obvious; for example, a narrow concentration on teaching a skill is not always the best way of achieving high standards in it.

6.2 The range of the curriculum at any time depends on the demands placed or felt to be placed upon schools. While all would presumably agree that it is essential that children are taught to read, write and calculate, few would regard this as sufficient. It is currently accepted that in the primary school children are taught to behave in socially and morally acceptable ways, to extend their spoken and written language and appreciation of literature, to comprehend mathematical and scientific ideas, to participate in a range of aesthetic and physical activities and, through their religious, moral, historical and geographical studies, to begin to see their own situation in a broader social context. It is therefore necessary to consider the range of learning which embodies these aims before making judgments about actual or desirable standards in any single part.

6.3 In an attempt to arrive at valid general descriptions of the range of the curriculum in the classes inspected, HMI used schedules (see Annex B) which they drew up before the main survey began. These listed the whole range of activities likely to be found in primary schools so that a record could be made within a single framework of what was done in any of the individual classes; the schedules were identical for all classes, no matter whether they were of 7, 9 or 11 year olds, and no matter what the special circumstances of a school. HMI expected teachers to be drawing from this wide range of items to suit the requirements of particular children or classes, to take local conditions into account or to make use of their own strengths.

6.4 Although, as had been assumed, individual classes did not undertake all of the items in the schedules it is nevertheless of interest to identify which items were taught to most children and were, therefore, by implication, those which a substantial percentage of teachers considered to be important. As a further step, it is then possible to establish what proportion of the classes covered the full range of items so identified. These are set out in the following paragraph. They do not represent a full range of curriculum which is considered desirable or even necessarily a minimum curriculum. They are merely items each of which was found to occur individually in at least 80 per cent of the survey classes[1].

6.5 These are the items so identified:

Language: listening and talking
(a) children were taught to
    i. follow instructions
    ii. follow the plot of a story
    iii. comprehend the main ideas in information given to them
(b) children talked informally to one another during the course of the working day
(c) discussion took place between children and teachers when new vocabulary was introduced.

Language: reading and writing
(a) in 7 and 9 year old classes children practised reading from a main reading scheme and from supplementary readers
(b) in 9 and 11 year old classes children read fiction and non-fiction which was not related to other work they were doing in the classroom
(c) in 11 year old classes children made use of information books related to work in other areas of the curriculum
(d) at each age children were encouraged to select books of their own choice
(e) children were given handwriting practice
(f) children undertook descriptive and narrative writing

[1] See Appendix G.

(g) in 9 and 11 year old classes children did written work on prescribed topics related to other parts of the curriculum.

Mathematics

Work was done to enable children to learn:

(a) to use language appropriate to the properties of number, size, shape and position

(b) to recognise relationships in geometrical shapes, numbers, ordered arrangements and everyday things

(c) to appreciate place value and recognise simpler number patterns

(d) to carry out suitable calculations involving $+$, $-$, $\times$ and $\div$ with whole numbers

(e) to understand money and the value of simple purchases

(f) to use numbers in counting, describing and estimating

(g) in 7 year old classes children undertook practical activities involving addition, subtraction, multiplication and division

In 11 year old classes children were taught to:

(h) estimate and use measurements of length, weight, area, volume and time

(i) work with the four rules of number including two places of decimals

(j) calculate using decimals

(k) use fractions, including the idea of equivalence, and apply them to everyday things

(l) use various forms of visual presentation including three dimensional and diagrammatic forms.

Aesthetic and physical education

The programme of work included:

(a) singing

(b) listening to music

(c) two or three dimensional work showing evidence of observation of pattern *or* colour *or* texture *or* form

(d) in 7 year old classes, practice of skills in gymnastics *or* games *or* swimming

(e) in 9 and 11 year old classes, gymnastic skills

(f) in 9 and 11 year old classes, practice of skills in playing games

(g) in 11 year old classes, swimming lessons.

Social abilities and moral learning

Work was arranged to promote the following:

(a) reliability and responsible attitudes

(b) consideration for other people; eg good manners, concern, friendship

(c) respect for surroundings and the care of materials and objects in the classroom and school

(d) participation as a member of a group or team, learning to follow rules and obey instructions

(e) involvement in the development of religious ideas and moral values during the school assembly

(f) in 9 and 11 year old classes, awareness of historical change and causal factors in relation to the way people lived or behaved in the past[1]

(g) in 9 and 11 year old classes, work relating to at least one of the following aspects of geography: population, agriculture, industry, transport, or resources within or outside the locality.[1]

6.6 The list invites certain obvious comments. Mention of teaching of the formal skills of spelling and syntax based on children's own writing does not appear because it occurred in too few classes. No single item relating to science could be included as, even when the items were grouped, as for geography, the percentage of classes undertaking any one of the items listed in the group did not reach 80 per cent.[2] The items (f) and (g) relating to history and geography do not allow a specific range of content to be identified within these subjects[3] and so no assumption can be made about whether or not any particular items are included in the programmes of all classes.

6.7 The coverage of items varied from class to class and showed no overall consistency. There was however 100 per cent coverage of some elements. Reading practice with a main reading scheme took place in every 7 year old class. Suitable calculations involving the four rules with whole numbers were practised in all classes at all ages.

6.8 A proportion of classes covered all the items under a given heading but it is not possible to generalise from one heading to the next. For example, in the case of mathematics, two-thirds of all the classes in the survey undertook work relating to all the items identified under that heading whereas in language work half of the classes were engaged in all the activities described, see Table 28. A more detailed description and assessment of the curriculum are given in Chapter 5.

6.9 When the range of work in more than one subject is considered, fewer than two-fifths of the classes at any age undertook work relating to all the identified items in both English language and mathematics. Moreover, when all the items for all subjects are considered together then less than a

---

[1] The incidence for this item in 9 and 11 year old classes was slightly below 80 per cent.
[2] See Chapter 5 iv
[3] See Chapter 5 vi.

third of the 7 year old classes, about a fifth of the 9 year old classes and a quarter of the 11 year old classes included all the activities, see Table 29. This would seem to suggest that in individual schools either some difficulty is found in covering appropriately the range of work widely regarded by teachers as worthy of inclusion in the curriculum, or that individual schools or teachers are making markedly individual decisions about what is to be taught based on their own perceptions and choices or a combination of these. Clearly ways of providing a more consistent coverage for important aspects of the curriculum need to be examined.

ii. STANDARDS AND THE CURRICULUM

Matching the standards of work to children's abilities

6.10 Teachers, parents and others are inevitably and rightly concerned with the standards achieved by children in school. It must, however, be recognised at the outset that there is no one standard which is appropriate to all children of a given age. Individual children vary in their capacities and abilities and some children perform moderately in one area of the curriculum and yet show good ability in another.

6.11 Class teachers were asked to identify, within their own classes, groups of more able, average and less able children. These categories related only to the range of abilities within the individual class and HM Inspectors did not try to establish any comparability between classes.

6.12 The relationship between the standard of work children in the groups were doing and that which they were considered by HMI to be capable of doing in each subject is referred to, for reasons of simplicity, as 'match'.[1] An assessment was made of the degree of match for each ability group within the class, in relation to each subject, on the basis of the standard of work the children were doing or had completed. A reasonably satisfactory match was recorded when the tasks presented to children were related to their existing skills and knowledge, when there was evidence of progression in the work and when there was evidence of the acquisition of further skill, information or understanding. When work was presented at the right level of difficulty children were normally confident and not afraid to make occasional errors which they regarded as a stimulus for further effort; in

---

[1] See Annex B

these circumstances children displayed a sense of purpose in their work and appeared to enjoy the challenge of the increasing, though realistic, demands made upon them[1].

The levels of match across the curriculum

6.13 In almost all the cases where work was not reasonably matched to children's capabilities, it was insufficiently demanding. It was very rare for children in any age or ability group to be required to undertake work which was too difficult for them. In the case of the most able groups at all three ages the work was considerably less well matched than for the average and less able groups. A clear pattern is discernible in the extent to which the work seen was reasonably matched to children's capabilities for different age and ability groups, see Tables 30–32.

6.14 The teaching of reading was most frequently judged to be reasonably matched with children's abilities for all ages and ability groups, although reading skills were less often extended appropriately for the most able groups, as compared with others, at all ages.

6.15 Following reading, the work in mathematics was most consistently recorded as reasonably matched to the children's ability for the average and less able groups. In the most able groups at all ages a reasonable match was achieved in only half of the classes for mathematics. The children in the most able groups were more frequently extended in their work in physical education than in their work in mathematics.

6.16 The work in reading, writing, spoken language, mathematics and physical education was more frequently judged to be reasonably matched to children's capabilities than work in other areas of the curriculum. Overall, about three-quarters of the average groups and rather more of the less able groups at all ages achieved a reasonable match in these subjects. But in respect of the more able groups the work in language, mathematics and physical education was reasonably matched in only about half of the classes.

6.17 The work in observational and experimental science was, at all ages and for each ability group, most commonly found to be less well matched to the children's capabilities than work in any other aspect

---

[1] See Chapter 5 and Annex B

of the curriculum. Children were not sufficiently challenged in over two-thirds of all groups. This lack of challenge occurred more frequently in the most able than in the less able groups.

6.18 Overall, the work in music and art and crafts was reasonably matched to children's abilities in these subjects in about half of all the classes, The work children did in music was consistently, for all abilities and ages, more frequently a reasonable match than the work in art and crafts. This probably reflects the special measures which were taken to assist the teaching of music: the allocation of positions of responsibility, the employment of peripatetic teachers of music and the use of teachers with musical skills to teach other classes[1]. These measures may also account for the better match of the work in music, relative to other subjects, for the most able pupils.

6.19 In geography and history the work was reasonably matched to children's capabilities in less than half of the classes. Elements of these subjects were frequently taught as topics or projects which sometimes resulted in repetitive work rather than an extension of children's skills and knowledge. The work in history and geography, except for the most able groups where there was considerable under-estimation of children's capacity at all ages, was more frequently reasonably matched to children's abilities in the 11 year old classes than for the younger children.

Observations on the levels found

6.20 The relative frequency with which the work in language and mathematics was reasonably matched to children's abilities reflects the high priority which these subjects were accorded in most schools. It may also be that levels of difficulty are better understood in these areas, partly perhaps because of the attention which they have received over the years; such attention was evidenced by the carefully graded reading and mathematics schemes in common use and the standardised tests which were administered in many schools[2].

6.21 In other subjects, with the exception of physical education, there was a widespread tendency to under-estimate the capacities of all groups of children, particularly the most able, in relation to the work they were

---

[1] See Chapters 3iii and 4i
[2] See Chapter 4i and ii

required to do. If children are to reach satisfactory standards in a full range of work within the curriculum there is a need to raise the general level of assumptions about what children are capable of doing and to establish sequences of learning in all subjects which will enable children to make progress and have confidence in their own abilities and capacities. There is also need for a realistic assessment of the range of work that can be covered within the context of the arrangements normally found in primary schools. This question is discussed in Chapter 8.

iii.   ATTAINMENTS IN READING AND MATHEMATICS

6.22 During the course of the survey, objective tests in reading and mathematics, administered by the National Foundation for Educational Research (NFER), were given to a sample of the children in the classes which were inspected. The details are given in Appendix I.

6.23 The children who were tested were randomly selected from the 9 and 11 year old classes. The 11 year old children were given reading test NS6 (National Survey Form Six) and mathematics test E2, which was a selection by specialist HMI of items produced by the NFER in connection with the Tests of Attainment in Mathematics in Schools Project; the items were chosen to produce a mean score of about 25 and for the range of attainment found among 11 year olds in the trial samples[1] of 1973 and in the pilot study. To assess the reading standards of the 9 year old children, reading test BD was used. A mathematics test was not administered to the 9 year old children.

6.24 Of the three tests, only for reading test NS6 were there previous surveys with which to compare the results of the present survey; these took place in 1955, 1960 and 1970. Reading standards for 9 year olds and standards in mathematics for 11 year olds have not previously been tested on a national scale, therefore no comparisons are possible.

6.25 In the present survey 4,955 11 year old children, drawn from 343[2] of the sample schools took the reading test NS6. The test is a sentence completion type in which the child has to choose the appropriate missing word from a selection which is offered. The items become progressively more difficult. An average score of 31.13 out of a possible 60 was obtained

---

[1] NFER trials of items for Tests of Attainment in Mathematics in Schools Project
[2] Tests from the remaining three schools could not be used, see Appendix E, paragraph 46

for the sample of 11 year old pupils. This is consistent with a rising trend in reading standards between 1955 and 1976–77.[1]

6.26 The reading test BD is of the same type as NS6. It was administered to 5,165 9 year old children in 372[2] of the sample schools. An average score of 20.13 out of a possible 44 was obtained but since this test had not previously been given to a national sample of 9 year olds there are no previous results with which comparisons can be made.[3] The 1976/77 results have been used to compare sub-groups of the sample.

6.27 A comparison of the boys' average NS6 scores with the girls' average NS6 scores shows no statistically significant difference at 11 years old. At 9 years of age, girls obtained a slightly higher average score on the BD reading test than the boys, though the top 10 per cent of the boys scored marginally higher than the top 10 per cent of the girls.

6.28 The 4,991 11 year olds who sat the mathematics test, E2, were drawn from 346 of the sample schools, ie all sample schools with 11 year olds. The test contains fifty items. Of these, ten were concerned with the properties of whole numbers, ten with handling everyday situations and ten with geometry; twelve dealt with graphical representation and the remaining eight were a miscellaneous group. The detailed statistical analysis of the results is shown in Appendix I. A mean total raw score was obtained of 27.97 out of 50 as compared with the anticipated score of about 25 (see paragraph 6.23); 10 per cent of the children scored more than 41 and 9.6 per cent scored 14 or less. There was no statistically significant difference in the total scores achieved by boys as compared with girls, though the boys did significantly better on the items concerned with graphical presentation.

6.29 Educational judgement, as well as statistical analysis, is required in interpreting the results of the test. It is hoped that the test items shown in Appendix I will help teachers and others to form a view of how well the children performed. Subjective examination by HM Inspectors of responses to the full test leads to the view that the results are disappointing in some respects when account is taken of the amount of time that is given to mathematics in primary schools.

6.30 There is a variety of reasons why children may fail to give a correct answer. Some children probably read questions incorrectly and a small

[1] See paragraphs 89–94, Appendix I
[2] Tests from the remaining three schools could not be used, see Appendix E, paragraph 46
[3] See paragraphs 95 and 96, Appendix I

number, judged by the NS6 results, could not read them at all. Even so, the test results may well indicate that between 10 and 15 per cent of children have difficulty in counting and adding accurately when using groups of tens and units. Some 60 to 70 per cent of children managed sums involving somewhat more complicated numbers, though some of these children may have been perplexed where they were required to produce two or more correct answers (see examples D and H); the percentage of correct responses falls noticeably where an unusual symbol is included (50 per cent of the schools appear not to introduce the ☐ of question G), or where there was need for a clear understanding of place value (particularly question H).

6.31 The responses to the two graphical items included in Appendix I may show that teaching too seldom goes beyond repetitive work on block graphs and is infrequently developed beyond this to the point where children become familiar with other forms of graphical presentation, eg linear graphs. On the other hand, the geometrical items shown were dealt with successfully by three-quarters or more of the children; others involving transformational symmetry or requiring an appreciation of changes of compass bearing were, not surprisingly, found more difficult.

6.32 Taking the test as a whole, it is clear that more children would have scored better if they had appreciated the general rules that can be seen operating in the large number of separate examples they work during mathematics lessons in schools, so that, for example, the answers to questions G and I could have been obtained by inspection.

Annex to Chapter 6

Table 28 The percentage of classes undertaking all widely taught items[1] in each subject and in social abilities

	7 year old classes	9 year old classes	11 year old classes
Mathematics	65	76	58
English language	54	43	53
Aesthetic and physical education	73	63	58
Social abilities	65	46	61

[1] These items, occurring in 80 per cent or more of the classes, are listed in paragraph 6.5.

Table 29 The percentage of classes undertaking all widely taught items[1] for combinations of two or more subjects

	7 year old classes	9 year old classes	11 year old classes
Items for English language and mathematics combined	42	37	39
Items for English language, mathematics and aesthetic and physical education combined	35	28	28
Items for English language, mathematics and social abilities combined	33	24	32
All items combined	29	19	24

[1] These items, occurring in 80 per cent or more of the classes, are listed in paragraph 6.5.

Table 30 Classes achieving reasonably satisfactory match for the average groups

Percentage of classes	Average groups		
	7 year old classes	9 year old classes	11 year old classes
94–85	Reading	Reading	–
84–75	Mathematics	Mathematics	Reading Mathematics
74–65	Physical education Writing Spoken language Music	Physical education Writing	Physical education Writing Spoken language
64–55	–	Spoken language Music	Music History
54–45	History Art and craft	History	Geography
44–35	Geography Science (observational)	Geography Art and craft	Art and craft Science (observational)
34–25	Science (experimental)	Science (observational)	Science (experimental)
24–20	–	Science (experimental)	–

Table 31   Classes achieving reasonably satisfactory match for less able groups

Percentage of classes	Less able groups		
	7 year old classes	9 year old classes	11 year old classes
94–85 84–75	Reading Mathematics Writing Spoken language Physical education	Reading Mathematics Writing	Reading Mathematics Writing
74–65	Music	Spoken language Physical education Music	Spoken language Physical education History
64–55	Art and craft	History	Music Geography
54–45	History Geography	Geography	Art and craft
44–35	Science (observational) Science (experimental)	Art and craft Science (observational)	Science (observational) Science (experimental)
34–25	–	Science (experimental)	–

Table 32   Classes achieving reasonably satisfactory match for most able groups

Percentage of classes	Most able groups		
	7 year old classes	9 year old classes	11 year old classes
64–55	Reading Physical education Spoken language	Reading Physical education	Reading Physical education
54–45	Mathematics Music Writing	Mathematics Music	Mathematics Music Spoken language
44–35	Art and craft	Writing Spoken language	Writing
34–25	History Geography	–	Art and craft History
24–15	Science (observational) Science (experimental)	Art and craft History Geography Science (observational)	Geography Science (observational) Science (experimental)
14–10	–	Science (experimental)	–

7 Associations between characteristics of the schools and classes and aspects of the children's work

i. GENERAL CONSIDERATIONS

7.1 The size of the sample used for this survey makes it possible to identify associations between some characteristics of the schools and classes and certain aspects of the children's work. These associations may reflect underlying causal relationships but this cannot be deduced from the information. Other unexamined factors undoubtedly affect the picture. Also, as information was collected at one point in time the survey is not a suitable vehicle for deciding which factors may be causes and which the effects. Specially designed studies would be necessary to throw light on whether the associations discussed in this chapter reflect causal relationships.[1]

7.2 Comparisons were made to establish whether the extent to which the children's work was well matched to their abilities varied with the length of the teaching experience of the class teacher. A breakdown of 1 up to 5 years, 5 up to 15 years, and 15 years or more of teaching experience was used. There were too few probationary teachers to include them. No differences were found in relating match to the length of teaching experience. Similarly the age range for which the teacher had initially trained was not found to be associated with the extent to which work was well matched to children's abilities. If the effect had been pronounced it would, no doubt, have been identified.[2]

ii. THE LOCALITY OF THE SCHOOL

7.3 Some factors remain the same, or much the same, during the period a

---

[1] See Annex to Chapter 7, Note 1.
[2] See Annex to Chapter 7, Note 2.

child is in the primary school. Most children remain in the same area and so the locality, and to a lesser extent the size and the type of school, whether a combined junior with infant school or separate junior and separate infant schools, are fairly constant factors. Of these, the locality of the school was found to be by far the most dominant characteristic.

Inner city schools

7.4 The average pupil teacher ratio in inner city schools was very similar to that in rural schools. The class size was larger because, unlike heads in small rural schools, the heads in inner city schools which, on average are larger, were not usually responsible for a class.[1] Also inner city schools were more likely to deploy teachers in other ways, including the withdrawal of groups of children from other classes for remedial purposes. Both the pupil teacher ratio and class size were generally more favourable in inner city schools than in schools in 'other urban' areas. The turnover of teachers was not noticeably higher in inner city schools than in other schools during the period for which information was collected[2] and, as in other schools, it tended to decline during that period.[3]

7.5 Resources and equipment were generally less satisfactory in inner city schools than in the schools in 'other urban' areas, although there were some schools in inner city areas which were particularly well equipped. The small number of schools inspected within any single local education authority area makes it impossible to distinguish whether these exceptions resulted from good management within an individual school or from provision by an authority because of special circumstances, for example the designation of some schools as being in social priority areas.

7.6 During the survey, three-fifths of the inner city schools were recorded as being in areas of marked social difficulty; though these schools are not necessarily those designated by local education authorities as being in social priority areas there is undoubtedly a fairly close correspondence. The more favourable pupil teacher ratio found in the schools recorded as being in areas of marked social difficulty seems to be a reflection of the allocation of additional resources to schools in social priority areas.[4] Perhaps surprisingly, these schools did not overall appear to receive more

[1] See Annex to Chapter 7, Note 3.
[2] See Annex to Chapter 7, Note 4.
[3] See Annex to Chapter 7, Note 5.
[4] See Annex to Chapter 7, Note 6.

time from peripatetic teachers or more non-teaching ancillary help than other schools.

Rural schools

7.7 A very substantial majority of the schools in rural areas were small, one form entry or less, combined junior with infant schools. The pupil teacher ratio in rural schools was very similar to that of inner city schools, though they were likely to have smaller classes with a wider age range of children within each class.[1] This is accounted for by the fact that in small rural schools, the teachers, including heads, almost all took responsibility for a class. While the turnover of teachers in rural schools was not noticeably different from that in other areas,[2] there were a number of small schools which had no changes of teacher during the period for which information was collected. Only a tenth of rural schools were classified as being in areas of marked social difficulty.

7.8 There was some evidence that, as compared with classes in inner city and 'other urban' areas, classes in rural schools paid more attention to spoken language. The teachers were more likely to read or tell stories to the children and the children in rural classes had more opportunity to talk informally to one another during the course of their work. The immediate outdoor environment of the school was used more often for educational purposes in rural classes than in others. Understandably, because of the distances and costs involved, rural classes made fewer visits to places such as museums or historical buildings.

7.9 Opportunities for some kinds of physical education were more limited in rural than in other schools. This was due partly to the small number of children of a given age, which made some forms of team games impracticable, and to the absence of a hall in a number of small schools, which reduced the opportunities for gymnastics and dance, particularly when poor weather limited the use of outdoor space.

Schools in 'other urban' areas

7.10 Schools in 'other urban' areas had a less favourable pupil teacher ratio and a larger average class size than schools in inner city or rural areas.[3]

[1] See Annex to Chapter 7, Note 3.
[2] See Annex to Chapter 7, Note 4.
[3] See Annex to Chapter 7, Note 3.

Schools in 'other urban' areas, which tended also to be larger schools, were rather better equipped, particularly for work in science, art and music, than schools in other areas. Music generally, and particularly singing, was given more emphasis in classes in 'other urban' schools than in others. There was also some evidence that these schools paid more attention to children's written work as a basis for learning language, including spelling, syntax and style, and as a means of monitoring children's progress in their English language work.

A comparison of NFER scores for classes in different localities[1]

7.11 Average NFER scores for classes of 9 and 11 year olds in inner city, 'other urban' and rural areas were compared.[2] The results indicate that the average reading scores for 9 and 11 year old classes and mathematics scores for 11 year old classes were significantly lower in classes in inner city schools than for classes in rural and 'other urban' schools.

7.12 A further analysis was carried out within each type of locality which indicated that these differences were not accounted for by the size or the type of school. In combined junior with infant schools 11 year old classes in inner city areas registered significantly lower reading and mathematics scores than classes in combined junior with infant schools in 'other urban' areas.

7.13 Assessments of the match between the work children were doing and that which they were considered capable of doing[3] were also compared for each locality. There were some indications that the work given to children in classes in inner city schools at 7, 9 and 11 years old was more likely to be too easy for them. However, these differences were not large enough to be statistically significant.

iii. TYPES OF SCHOOL

7.14 Most separate junior and separate infant schools were two form entry or larger and were mainly found in inner city and 'other urban' areas.

---

[1] *NFER scores* refers to reading test NS6 at 11 years old, reading test BD at 9 years old and mathematics test E2 at 11 years old. (See Chapter 6iii and Appendix I).
[2] See Annex to Chapter 7, Note 7.
[3] See Chapter 6ii and Annex Tables 30–32.

Small, one form entry or less, combined junior with infant schools predominated in rural areas and were rarely found in 'other urban' areas.[1] These overlapping factors have to be borne in mind when comparing one type of school with another. In order to exclude as far as possible differences arising from locality and size, only two-form entry schools were considered when comparing types of school. Two-form entry schools were distributed in reasonably similar proportions among different school types within each locality and were sufficiently numerous to allow analysis.[2]

7.15 Taking 'other urban' and rural areas together, the curriculum of the 7 and 11 year olds in separate junior and separate infant schools was more likely to cover a broad range of the widely taught items in mathematics than that of the 7 and 11 year olds classes in combined junior with infant schools.[3] The same was true of geography and history for 9 and 11 year old classes in separate junior schools. On the other hand, children of 9 and 11 years of age in combined junior with infant schools made more use of three dimensional constructional materials, although 7 year old classes in separate infant schools were likely to be better equipped for work in art and crafts.

7.16 There were no significant differences in the NFER scores for children of 9 and 11 years of age in the different types of schools. Overall, only slight differences were found when comparing the work of children in combined junior with infant schools with those in separate infant and separate junior schools. In general, the differences between individual schools were more marked than any systematic differences attributable to the size or type of school.

iv.   ORGANISATION OF CLASSES AND ARRANGEMENTS FOR TEACHING

Size of class

7.17 In order to examine the association of class size with NFER mean

---

[1] See Annex to Chapter 2, Table 3.

[2] The size of a school is defined as form of entry and not the total number of children on roll. A two-form entry infant school has fewer children on roll than a two-form entry combined junior with infant school.

[3] 'Widely taught items' refers to those items occurring in 80 per cent or more of the classes listed in Chapter 6i, paragraph 5.

scores, the classes of 11 year olds were grouped into size bands.[1] This preliminary analysis appears to indicate that the larger the class size, the better the NFER reading scores.

7.18 However, it was known from previous analysis[2] that the locality of the school was an important factor in influencing test performance. The comparisons were therefore repeated for each locality separately.[3] This analysis too seems to indicate a slight positive relationship between increasing class size and NFER scores in inner city schools but not in the other localities. Overall, for the 11 year olds, there was no evidence of a consistent relationship between class size and improved NFER reading scores. Similarly, no firm trends were identified in the analysis of mathematics scores at 11 years old or reading scores at 9 years old.

The age range of classes

7.19 Some schools have so few pupils and teachers that they have no choice but to arrange children in classes which cover more than one school year group. Other schools have sufficient classes to separate the age groups but may prefer not to do so. In some cases these 'mixed age' classes amount to no more than an arrangement to keep the numbers in classes fairly even; in other instances the mixture of age groups is deliberate policy and is often referred to as vertical or 'family' grouping.[4]

7.20 When match assessments[5] were compared for single age and 'mixed age' classes it was found that for 7 and 11 year olds the single age classes showed a definite superiority in relating the difficulty of the work to children's capabilities at all ability levels. The 11 year olds in single age classes also produced better NFER scores for reading and mathematics than children in 'mixed age' classes. For 9 year old children there was no significant difference in the match assessments, although single age classes tended to show slightly better match than mixed age classes; the difference in NFER scores, though smaller than with the 11 year olds, favoured single age classes and was statistically significant.[6] This may reflect the fact that 9 year old children were to be found in classes with either younger or older

---

[1] See Annex to Chapter 7, Note 8.
[2] See Annex to Chapter 7, Note 7.
[3] See Annex to Chapter 7, Note 9.
[4] See Chapter 3i, Figures 6 and 7.
[5] See Chapter 6ii and Annex Tables 30–32.
[6] See Annex to Chapter 7, Note 10.

children, while 7 and 11 year olds in 'mixed age' classes were normally placed with children of a younger age range.

7.21 The survey did not include classes for children of 5 and 6 years old for whom vertical grouping is sometimes introduced to overcome the problems arising from taking new children into the school each term. Termly entry may result in children being transferred to a new class after only a few months, and in these circumstances the advantages of continuity in the same class may well outweigh any disadvantages arising from an increased age range within the class. However, in view of the findings relating to 7 year olds, it would appear that a single age class has advantages for these pupils and that teachers are better able to match the difficulty of work to their capabilities, at all ability levels, in a single age class than when they are placed in a vertically grouped class with younger children.

Streaming of classes by ability

7.22 The proportion of classes streamed by ability at 11 years of age was too small to form a group which could reliably be compared with 'mixed ability' classes.[1] However, when the NFER scores in reading and mathematics for the streamed classes were omitted from the calculations there was virtually no change in the average scores obtained by 11 year old children.

Grouping by ability within a class

7.23 The number of classes where children were grouped by ability for their work in English language and mathematics was so large that no reliable comparison could be made with other classes in which children were not grouped by ability.[2]

Individual assignments of work

7.24 The use of individual assignments of work for English language and mathematics, whether presented by the teacher or through the use of text books or assignment cards, was so common in 11 year old classes that no reliable comparison could be made with classes in which teachers did not

---

[1] See Annex to Chapter 3, Table 12.
[2] See Annex to Chapter 3, Table 15.

employ this method of organising work.[1] In 9 year old classes the work was slightly better matched to children's abilities in these subjects where it was presented by individual assignments, but the position was reversed for the 7 year old classes.

v. TEACHING METHODS AND RANGE OF WORK

7.25 A broad categorisation of teaching approaches observed in the survey is described in Chapter 3v. Teachers in a minority of classes employed a combination of didactic and exploratory approaches; in these classes the work children were given to do was better matched to their capabilities for the least, average and most able than in those classes using mainly didactic or mainly exploratory methods.

7.26 In the smallest group of classes, one in twenty, which relied on a mainly exploratory approach the children scored less well in the NFER tests in reading and mathematics. There was also some indication that the work was least well matched to the children's abilities in these classes although the number of classes involved was too small for formal analysis.

7.27 In classes where a didactic approach was mainly used, better NFER scores were achieved for reading and mathematics than in those classes using mainly exploratory approaches. The NFER scores for the group of classes using mainly didactic approaches were only marginally lower than for the children in the classes using a combination of exploratory and didactic methods; the difference was not statistically significant.

7.28 A quiet working atmosphere was established whenever necessary in a very substantial majority of the classes in each of the three age groups. In the small number of classes where this did not happen the work was less well matched to the children's capabilities at all ages for all ability levels. In the case of 9 and 11 year olds, the average NFER scores for children in these classes compared poorly with those of the children in the majority of classes.

7.29 In connection with children's NFER scores in reading and mathematics a wide range of variables was tested. All which showed a strong association with higher scores are mentioned here. Predictably, variables

---

[1] See Annex to Chapter 3, Table 14.

tended to cluster and classes which made use of one variable tended also to undertake activities relating to others.

7.30 Higher average NFER reading scores for 9 year olds were associated with those classes where children made good use of book collections or libraries and, in the case of 11 year olds, with those using good quality work cards. Stories and poems were read to children in a higher proportion of the classes with above average NFER reading scores than in other classes.

7.31 Better average NFER scores in mathematics were associated with those 11 year old classes where skills were regularly practised from the blackboard. In these classes attention was also likely to be given to the recognition of mathematical relationships. More of these classes made use of visual presentation including models, maps and scale drawings, and the children practised calculations involving the four rules of number applied to whole numbers, decimals and fractions. Better average NFER scores were also associated with those classes where children undertook practical activities, as well as calculations, involving the four rules of number.

7.32 It should not however be assumed that increasing the practice in relation to one particular activity necessarily improves the children's performance. The indications are rather that giving reasonable attention to a range of different activities is more likely to be effective.

7.33 It was found that children in those 9 and 11 year old classes which covered most of the widely taught items[1] achieved better average NFER reading and mathematics scores than children in other classes where the coverage was less broad.[2] In these classes the work was also better matched to the children's capacities for all abilities in each age group. This would seem to suggest that in those classes where a reasonable coverage of widely taught items was achieved, the work was more likely to be pitched at the right level for the abilities of the children and that this, in turn, was associated with higher NFER scores for reading and mathematics.

vi. TEACHERS WITH SPECIAL RESPONSIBILITIES

7.34 Over half the 9 and 11 year old classes and two-fifths of the 7 year

---

[1] 'Widely taught items' refers to those items occurring in 80 per cent or more of the classes listed in Chapter 6i, paragraph 5.
[2] See Annex to Chapter 7, Note 11.

old classes were taught music by a teacher other than their own class teacher.[1] In the case of music, when other teachers undertake this task this is usually because they have some degree of expertise in this subject which the class teacher does not have. In 9 and 11 year old classes the work in music was better matched to the children's capabilities where they were taught by another teacher than in those classes of the same age taught music by their own class teacher. This was not the case in 7 year old classes.

7.35 Lastly, a comparison was carried out to see whether there was an association between the degree of influence of teachers holding posts which carried special responsibilities in the school and the work of the children.[2]

7.36 A 'match rating' was calculated for each class and it was found that where teachers who held posts carrying special responsibilities had a strong influence in the school this was very strongly associated with good match for all ages and all abilities.[3] This was particularly noticeable in the case of the most able children where the work was considerably better matched to their abilities when teachers with special responsibilities had a strong influence in the school.

7.37 These findings suggest that where a teacher with a special responsibility is knowledgeable and able to give a strong lead in planning and carrying out a programme of work, this is effective in influencing the work of other teachers in the school. This in turn would appear to raise the levels of expectations of what children are capable of doing, particularly in relation to the most able children, who were often the least likely to be given work which would extend them intellectually.

Annex to Chapter 7

Note 1

The associations described in this chapter were tested by the application of contingency table analysis and analysis of variance. (See Appendix G.)

---

[1] See Annex to Chapter 3, Table 20.
[2] See Chapter 2ii and 4i.
[3] See Annex to Chapter 7, Note 12.

Note 2

Over three-quarters of teachers were teaching an age range for which they originally trained.[1] Comparisons were made with match assessments to establish whether there were differences when teachers were teaching an age range other than that for which they had originally trained. These comparisons were made separately for teachers with up to 5 years teaching experience and those with 5 or more years experience. No differences were found in terms of the extent to which work was matched to children's capabilities for each ability level; it must be recognised that children's present performance owes much to previous teaching they have received.

Note 3

(a) The pupil teacher ratio in each locality[2]

Schools teaching children of this age	Inner city	'Other urban'	Rural
7 years	22.5	24.2	23.0
9 years	23.2	25.5	23.4
11 years	23.4	25.5	23.3

(b) The average size of class in each locality[2]

Schools teaching children of this age	Inner city	'Other urban'	Rural
7 years	28.5	30.3	26.9
9 years	29.8	31.6	28.1
11 years	31.9	32.8	28.5

[1] See Chapter 2ii and Annex to Chapter 2, Table 6.
[2] Based on unweighted data.

Note 4

Percentage of all teachers by the length of time in their present school for each locality

	Inner city	'Other urban'	Rural	All localities
Less than 1 year	16	15	16	16
1 up to 5 years	49	48	45	47
5 up to 15 years	27	30	31	29
More than 15 years	8	7	8	8

Note : Measurement was on the basis of completed terms. Hence less than one year implies two or fewer completed terms.
Another analysis, based on staff movements in individual schools, was inconclusive because it required too much sub-division of the sample. There was, however, no strong evidence that inner city schools had experienced higher turnover.

Note 5

The proportion of teachers with less than one year's experience and the proportion of teachers who had been at their present school for less than a year were taken as indicators of teacher turnover. Comparisons were made for each of the five terms covered by the survey.

	Schools inspected in autumn term 1975	Schools inspected in spring term 1976	Schools inspected in summer term 1976	Schools inspected in autumn term 1976	Schools inspected in spring term 1977	All Schools
% of teachers with less than one years teaching experience	18	15	17	14	14	16
% of teachers at present school for less than one year	7	5	6	3	4	5

Note : In both cases measurement was on the basis of the number of completed terms. Hence less than one year implies two or fewer completed terms.

Note 6

The pupil teacher ratio for schools in areas of marked social difficulty.[1]

Age of children	Schools with marked social difficulties	Other schools, including small schools
7 years	22.4	23.7
9 years	23.4	24.7
11 years	23.5	24.6

Note 7

A comparison of NFER mean scores (unweighted) for each locality shows the following results:

Locality	Reading Test BD	Reading Test NS6	Mathematics Test E2
Inner city	17.9	27.9	24.5
'Other urban'	20.3	32.0	28.3
Rural	20.7	30.6	28.3

[1] Based on unweighted data.

Note 8

NS6 Reading Test Scores for 11 year olds by size of class

	Number of children in the class								
	20 or less		21 to 25		26 to 30		31 to 35		36 or more	
	Number of classes	Mean score	Number of classes	Mean score	Number of classes	Mean score	Number of classes	Mean score	Number of classes	Mean score
	20	27.9	39	29.7	76	29.2	130	31.6	76	32.3

Note 9

NS6 Reading Test Scores for 11 year olds by size of class for each locality

	Number of children in the class									
Locality	20 or less		21 to 25		26 to 30		31 to 35		36 or more	
	Number of classes	Mean Score	Number of classes	Mean Score	Number of classes	Mean Score	Number of classes	Mean Score	Number of classes	Mean Score
Inner city	–	–	9[1]	23.2	13	26.5	19	29.6	17	29.6
'Other urban'	2	27.1	10	31.8	33	30.2	78	32.2	41	33.2
Rural	17	28.7	21	30.9	30	29.4	33	31.4	18	32.8

[1] One inner city class falls into the 20 or less band and 8 fall into the 21 to 25 band. The analysis requires a minimum of 2 entries in a cell. Hence the 9 classes have been grouped together in the 21–25 band.

Note 10

For the purposes of this analysis all classes of 25 or fewer children were excluded.

The maximum size of the age group, within 'mixed age' classes of 26 to 36 or more pupils, was set at 15. Thus 'mixed age' and single age classes were defined as follows:

'Mixed age' classes		Single age classes[1]	
Class size	Size of relevant age group	Class size	Size of relevant age group
26–30	6–15	26–30	26–30
31–35	6–15	31–35	31–35
36 or more	6–15	36 or more	36 or more

This ensured that no effects due to very small classes obscured the analysis and that a clear distinction between the two types of class organisation was preserved.

---

[1] A maximum of five children in a different age group was allowed.

Note 10

NFER Scores for mixed age and single age classes

	Number of classes	Mean score for these classes	Standard error	Difference of means (single age— mixed age)	Conclusion
11 years olds **NS6 reading test:**					
Single age	199	31.61	5.26 ⎫		Single age mean
Mixed age	29	26.88	6.55 ⎭	4.73	score higher than mixed age classes mean
E2 mathematics test:					
Single age	199	28.09	4.90 ⎫		Single age mean
Mixed age	29	24.95	7.29 ⎭	3.14	score higher than mixed age classes mean
9 year olds **BD reading test**					
Single age	187	20.38	4.23 ⎫		Single age mean
Mixed age	51	18.97	5.04 ⎭	1.41	score higher than mixed age classes mean

Note 11

Classes which undertook work relating to all the items listed for language[1] had a higher mean score for reading test BD at 9 years old and reading test NS6 at 11 years old. Similarly classes undertaking all the items listed for mathematics[1] achieved a higher mean score on test E2 at 11 years. Classes which undertook work relating to all the items listed for language, mathematics, aesthetics and social studies[1] had higher average NFER scores for reading at 9 years and reading and mathematics at 11 years. In the groups obtaining the best match assessments for each subject the proportion of classes undertaking work related to all the widely taught items for each subject was as follows: in mathematics 83 per cent, in language 88 per cent and in aesthetics 89 per cent. There was a very strong association between good match and undertaking work in all the widely taught items, both for each individual subject and for the whole curriculum. Social studies could not be tested for this association since the widely taught items and match assessments did not correspond.

Note 12

'Match ratings' were calculated as follows[2]:

Considerable over expectation		1
Slight over expectation	⎫ reasonably good	2
Good match	⎬ match	3
Slight under expectation	⎭	2
Considerable under expectation		1

In practice virtually no over expectation was recorded, so a low match rating implied under expectation. Rating groups were chosen on statistical grounds and can be interpreted as follows:

Group ratings

a.   lower match rating (increased degree of under expectation)

b. ⎫
c. ⎬ intermediate match ratings

d.   higher match rating (higher frequency of good and reasonably good match).

---

[1] See Chapter 6 i, paragraph 5
[2] See Appendix G

The number of 7 year old classes, for each ability group, by the degree of influence of teachers holding posts of special responsibility in the school, falling into each match rating group

7 year old classes	Match rating group		Teachers with posts of responsibility in the school have:			All Classes
			Strong influence	Some influence	Little influence	
Most able children	a.	lower	2	25	154	181
	b.	intermediate	6	21	78	105
	c.		2	18	33	53
	d.	higher	16	21	28	65
	Total		26	85	293	404
Average ability children	a.	lower	0	7	84	91
	b.	intermediate	3	13	75	91
	c.		4	19	64	87
	d.	higher	19	46	70	135
	Total		26	85	293	404
Less able children	a.	lower	0	2	59	61
	b.	intermediate	1	12	65	78
	c.		3	13	73	89
	d.	higher	22	58	96	176
	Total		26	85	293	404

The number of 9 year old classes, for each ability group, by the degree of influence of teachers holding posts of special responsibility in the school, falling into each match rating group

9 year old classes	Match rating group		Teachers with posts of responsibility in the school have:			All Classes
			Strong influence	Some influence	Little influence	
Most able children	a.	lower	1	22	183	206
	b. }	intermediate	3	16	58	77
	c. }		3	18	29	50
	d.	higher	11	15	14	40
	Total		18	71	284	373
Average ability children	a.	lower	0	10	91	101
	b. }	intermediate	2	10	84	96
	c. }		3	16	68	87
	d.	higher	13	35	41	89
	Total		18	71	284	373
Less able children	a.	lower	0	7	55	62
	b. }	intermediate	0	8	92	100
	c. }		2	17	75	94
	d.	higher	16	39	62	117
	Total		18	71	284	373

Note 12 (c)

The number of 11 year old classes, for each ability group, by the degree of influence of teachers holding posts of special responsibility in the school, falling into each match rating group

11 year old classes	Match rating group		Teachers with posts of responsibility in the school have:			All Classes
			Strong influence	Some influence	Little influence	
Most able children	a.	lower	1	16	146	163
	b. }	intermediate	1	21	60	82
	c. }		3	7	40	50
	d.	higher	10	22	17	49
	Total		15	66	263	344
Average ability children	a.	lower	0	4	62	66
	b. }	intermediate	1	17	68	86
	c. }		0	10	71	81
	d.	higher	14	35	62	111
	Total		15	66	263	344
Less able children	a.	lower	0	3	39	42
	b. }	intermediate	0	12	66	78
	c. }		0	14	68	82
	d.	higher	15	37	90	142
	Total		15	66	263	344

8 The main findings, issues and recommendations

8.1 In the course of this survey a number of questions have been posed about the work done in primary schools: what activities occur and with what emphasis; is the work well suited to the capacities of the children; and how well do children perform on certain objective tests? In addition, observations have been made of the ways in which children behave in school, and heads and teachers have supplied information on the forms of organisation used and on other matters.

8.2 A further question raised by the report is: what should now be done to develop primary education further so that the educational requirements of children and the changing needs of society as a whole are met as nearly as they can be? In this chapter some of the main findings of the report are considered with this question in mind. Section i, *The general setting for the work*, is concerned with the conditions in which learning takes place and with the general organisation of primary schools; Section ii, *The curriculum*, is about the work of the children; Section iii, *Class and specialist teaching*, discusses the deployment of teachers; Section iv, *The professional development of teachers*, deals with the implications of the report for initial and in-service training.

8.3 Passages containing recommendations and main issues for consideration by teachers and others are italicised.

i. THE GENERAL SETTING FOR THE WORK

8.4 Typically, the children are divided into classes according to age, not ability, though a substantial number of classes contain children from more than one year group. Most classes contain between twenty and thirty-five children. The smaller classes are commonly in the smaller schools, usually in rural areas where some contain fewer than twenty children, and are the most likely to have children from two or more age groups.[1]

8.5 The teacher in charge of a class teaches it for most of the programme of work. The class teacher may well exchange classes with another member of staff who specialises in music, and take the latter's class for some aspect of English. The older the children, the greater the chance that there is specialist teaching for music and for other purposes, but even the teacher in charge of the 11 year olds usually teaches the class for nearly the whole week.[2]

8.6 The children behave responsibly and cooperate with their teacher and with other children.[3] Discussion takes place between teachers and children and amongst children. A quiet working atmosphere is established when necessary. *In the few classes where this is not established the children are not likely to be making the progress they should; inattentiveness in school and low scores in the objective tests are both associated with a failure to provide work of a suitable level of difficulty.*[4]

8.7 Teachers clearly attach great importance to children learning to live together amicably and gaining a sense of social responsibility. Children are taught to be considerate towards other people and to respect their surroundings. Teachers are usually quick to use incidents which arise throughout the school day to draw children's attention to general moral and social issues.[5]

The organisation of schools and falling rolls

8.8 When this survey took place, the number of children in primary schools, except in inner city and some well-established new town areas, had not dropped substantially. The fall in the birth rate, which has already taken place, will produce a much larger reduction of numbers in the next few years; some schools will be closed and, elsewhere, the internal organisation of schools will be affected. Some findings of the survey are relevant to these changes.

---

[1] See Chapters 3 i and 7 iv
[2] See Chapter 3 iii
[3] See Chapter 5 i
[4] See Chapter 7 v, paragraph 28
[5] See Chapter 5 i

8.9 There were signs that schools of two form entry or larger were likely to be better equipped than smaller schools. In particular, children in infant schools, which tend to have at least two forms of entry, were better provided for in music and art[1] ; large schools in 'other urban' areas generally had better resources for science.[2] The survey did not investigate ways in which schools were funded, but it is well known that local education authorities provide schools with equipment and materials not only through capitation allowances, but also through additional grants because a school is small in size, or for some particular curricular purpose, or through the provision of common services, such as the school library service. *The implications of the survey are that the balance between capitation allowances and these additional resources at present favours the larger school, and, especially if the average size of school is to become smaller, there may be good reasons for re-examining this balance. It has also to be recognised, however, that the small advantages in the levels of resources of large schools did not appear to improve the performance of their pupils other than marginally in art and music.*[3]

8.10 As school rolls fall, the number of classes may have to be reduced. This could lead to there being more classes of mixed age ranges than previously. There is clear evidence from the survey that the performance of children in these circumstances can suffer.[4] *There may be advantage in combining separate infant schools and combining separate junior schools if doing so allows the formation of classes of single age groups, though other factors such as the extent of the catchment area also have to be taken into account.*

8.11 High and low levels of performance were much more strongly associated with the location of the school as defined in this survey[5] than with either the size of the school (as indicated by forms of entry) or its age range. It made no significant difference in terms of work and performance whether children were in a separate junior or separate infant school or in a combined infant with junior school.[6] *When schools are closed because of falling rolls, there does not seem to be, overall, any significant educational advantage in changing, during the course of reorganisation, from separate infant and separate junior schools to combined primary schools.*

---

[1] Chapter 7 iii, paragraph 15
[2] Chapter 7 ii, paragraph 10
[3] Chapter 7 iii
[4] Chapter 7 iv, paragraphs 19–21
[5] Chapter 7 ii, paragraphs 11–13
[6] Chapter 7 iii

Resources and school buildings

8.12 The survey was primarily concerned with the content of the children's work and their levels of performance. Resources were considered in relation to these factors and some mention of resources has been made incidentally in the report.[1]

8.13 The survey took place in circumstances that were changing and continue to change. The effects of restraint in public expenditure on books, materials and equipment had not yet fully worked through to the school system and schools were still benefiting, to some extent, from purchases made before the rate of inflation was at its peak.

8.14 About one-fifth of the classes were found to be working in conditions that inhibited, to some degree, the range of work.[2] The most common shortcoming was that of space and this deficiency may be alleviated, as numbers fall, if the space available can be well used for the fewer children. *Such use may depend as much on staffing levels as on decisions to close schools or to use spare accommodation for other purposes, as most teaching space is still in the form of individual classrooms, each of which requires separate supervision.*

8.15 *More spare classrooms could be used for activities which require a substantial amount of space and special equipment, for example, science, craft, art or drama. The use of otherwise spare rooms for music would free halls for additional indoor physical education.* There are some small schools, usually in rural areas, which do not have a hall. Opportunities for indoor physical education in these schools may be severely restricted, but it cannot automatically be assumed that the first priority for such schools is that they should have a hall added to them; much depends of the accommodation, on the outside facilities already available and on the ability of teachers to compensate for the lack of a large unencumbered space, and on the other needs of the school.[3]

---

[1] Chapters 2 iii, 5 and 7 ii & iii
[2] Chapter 2 iii, paragraph 17
[3] Chapter 5 v

ii. THE CURRICULUM

The basic skills

8.16 High priority is given to teaching children to read, write and learn mathematics.[1]

8.17 The teaching of reading is regarded by teachers as extremely important,[2] and the basic work in this skill is undertaken systematically. *The levels of ability of the children inevitably vary, but those who find learning to read difficult are more likely to be given work suitably matched to their abilities than the children who are more able readers.*[3]

8.18 The survey also makes it possible to say, on the basis of the scores in the NFER reading test, NS6, that the results of surveys conducted since 1955 are consistent with gradually improving reading standards of 11 year olds.[4] It is only in the reading performance of 11 year olds that earlier data exist for statistical comparisons to be made with the findings of this survey.

8.19 *It is vital that the careful work already being done to ensure that children become literate should continue and be further developed. Future marked improvement in the general level of performance in reading, however, probably depends on developing a more systematic approach to teaching average and more able readers to find the books they require and to use the contents page and index to decide whether to skim or to study a text thoroughly; to follow a line of argument critically; and to look out for the implications of what is written, as well as to note the explicit information the passage contains. For this to be achieved children need to be introduced to a wide range of reading material in connection with many aspects of their work.*[5]

8.20 In writing, considerable effort is made to teach syntax and spelling.[6] *It may be that because this work is often based on isolated exercises, the rules are too often forgotten when children write in their own words, as they frequently have the opportunity to do. What is written is often descriptive or narrative in form and, while these forms are important, by*

---

[1] Chapter 6 ii
[2] Chapter 5 ii
[3] Chapter 6 ii
[4] Chapter 6 iii and Appendix I
[5] Chapter 5 ii
[6] Chapter 5 ii

11 years of age more children might be expected to develop an argument or to explore an idea when writing than is now the case. Furthermore, the time spent on writing should allow for the correction and improvement of initial attempts.

8.21 The children spend a considerable amount of time on mathematics and the work in this subject is better matched to their abilities than is the work in most other subjects – though the more able children often work at too low a level. In the light of these efforts, the scores achieved in the NFER mathematics test, E2, are disappointing.[1]

8.22 *It seems clear from this part of the survey that individual assignments should not be allowed to replace all group or class work in mathematics.*[2] *Teachers can, by working regularly with a group or the whole class, quicken the pace of mental response and encourage accuracy. They may also, in these circumstances, more readily draw children's attention to general rules in the work they do and so help to create a better under-standing of the ways in which numbers behave. Children need to practise mental and written calculations in the four rules of number, including whole numbers and, when they are ready, decimals and fractions. They also need to use numbers in connection with practical activities. The forms of questions and the forms of answers required ought to be varied so that children are not put off by an unusual word, or combination of words or symbols. More of the examples worked by children could usefully lead to multiple answers.*[3] *The work in mathematics should not be confined to the four rules of number: children in those classes where the programme included all mathematical items taught to 80 per cent of classes for the age group did better in the mathematics test.*[4]

8.23 *The evidence of the survey bears out the view that the effective application of skills, including their use in practical activities, is important. The teaching of skills in isolation, whether in language or in mathematics, does not produce the best results.*[5]

---

[1] Chapter 6 ii & iii and Appendix I
[2] Chapter 7 iv & v
[3] Chapter 6 iii and Appendix I
[4] Chapter 6 i, paragraph 5
[5] Chapter 7 v, paragraphs 31–33

Other aspects of the curriculum

8.24 The curriculum as a whole provides many opportunities for pupils to apply basic skills, and it contains other elements that are important in their own right. The programme of most classes included work on plants, animals and man-made objects and materials. The children were taught about the historical and geographical context of the society in which they live, and the moral values that underlie it. Unless their parents asked for them to be withdrawn, they took part in religious education based on Christian beliefs.[1] *More might be done to make all children aware of other beliefs and to extend their understanding of the multi-cultural nature of contemporary society. In the course of work on these and other matters, children acquire information and learn to respond imaginatively to what they see, hear and otherwise experience.*

8.25 *Curricular content should be selected not only to suit the interests and abilities of the children and to provide for the progressive development of the basic skills, but also because it is important in its own right.* This requires a considerable knowledge of the subject material, going far beyond that which is to be used explicitly in the classroom. The teacher's need for a thorough knowledge of the subject becomes more marked as the children get older.

8.26 *Observed practices in some parts of the curriculum show the difficulty that a considerable proportion of teachers have in selecting and utilising subject matter. Science is the outstanding example[2] and one in which no individual item of observational or experimental work occurred in as many as 80 per cent of the classes at any age[3]; this is only the aspect of the curriculum of which this is true. Craft is also making a smaller contribution to the work than is desirable.[4] The lack of progression and the amount of repetition in the work in geography and history probably result from a lack of planning, though the mere presence of a scheme of work is no guarantee that a subject is well taught; over 40 per cent of the schools had schemes of work in science but there was little evidence of these programmes being implemented.[5]*

8.27 Physical education was given about as high a priority as mathematics.

[1] Chapter 5 i & vi
[2] Chapter 5 iv
[3] Chapter 6 ii, paragraph 6
[4] Chapter 5 v
[5] Chapter 4, Table 25

Music, of which more will be said later, was also given relatively high priority. *It is interesting to notice that both of these subjects were among those for which there were frequently teachers with posts of responsibility.*[1]

The range of the curriculum

8.28 It might be argued that if some parts of the curriculum are difficult for class teachers to deal with it would be better to narrow the range of the curriculum. That view does not seem to be borne out by the findings of this survey. The basic skills are more successfully learnt when applied to other subjects[2] and children in the classes which covered a full range of the widely taught items[3] did better on the NFER tests at 9 and 11 years of age; also, for all three age groups the work of children in these classes was better matched to their abilities than was the work of children in other classes. This finding has to be interpreted with care, because the remaining classes did not necessarily have narrower curricula; the teachers may merely have been more idiosyncratic in their choice of items. *Nevertheless, there is no evidence in the survey to suggest that a narrower curriculum enabled children to do better in the basic skills or led to the work being more aptly chosen to suit the capacities of the children.*

8.29 *The general educational progress of children and their competence in the basic skills appear to have benefited where they were involved in a programme of work that included art and craft, history and geography, music and physical education, and science, as well as language, mathematics and religious and moral education, although not necessarily as separate items on a timetable.*[4] *There is no justification for differentiation between the curriculum for boys and for girls because of traditional differences in social roles; such differentiation as does still occur, for example in craft work which limits girls to using soft materials, is unusual and should cease.*[5]

8.30 *It remains important to establish priorities and to keep the curriculum within realistic limits. Agreement on these matters should be sought far more than is now done with other schools in the locality, primary and secondary, and in accordance with national needs.*[6]

[1] Chapters 6 ii and 4 i, Table 24
[2] Chapter 7 v
[3] Chapter 6 i, paragraph 5
[4] Annex to Chapter 7, Note 11
[5] Chapter v paragraph 95
[6] Chapter 4 iii.

8.31 *Such agreement makes it easier to ensure that the programmes of primary and secondary schools are attuned, and that there is continuity as children move from one stage to the next.*

Differences amongst children within a class

8.32 Especially in the basic skills, but also in other parts of the curriculum, children are frequently divided into groups, or provided with individual assignments of work. In the basic skills, the main objective is to give work that is of an appropriate level of difficulty. In some other parts of the curriculum the groups are based on common interests or on friendship. The almost universal occurrence of grouping and individual work indicate the concern that teachers have for individual children.[1]

8.33 The evidence of the survey shows that children's needs are more successfully catered for in some parts of the curriculum than in others; and throughout the curriculum, the needs of some children are more often met than are the needs of others. *The relative success that teachers have in matching the work in the basic skills for the slower children has already been mentioned in this chapter[2]. Otherwise, it is broadly the case that the more able children within a class were the least likely to be doing work that was sufficiently challenging.*

8.34 One reason may be that it is difficult for a teacher to keep track of what every child in a class is doing if each is engaged in a different activity. *Certainly children who were customarily given some — though not too much — mathematical instruction in groups working from the blackboard with their teacher were at an advantage in completing the NFER test[3].* This advantage may have come about because a teacher could afford to spend more time explaining a process to a group than to a series of individuals, or because the group contact enabled the teacher to inject more pace into the work, or because the children learnt from each other's questions, or all three. *Some potential loss of precision in matching the work to individuals was compensated for by other factors; in practice, the loss of precision in the grading of work for groups as compared with individuals may be negligible.*

---

[1] Chapter 3 ii, paragraphs 5–8 and Annex to Chapter 3, Tables 14 and 15.
[2] Annex to Chapter 6, Tables 30–32
[3] Chapter 7 v, paragraph 31

8.35 Another reason why teachers find it more difficult to match the level of work to the abler than to the slower children in their classes may be that these children are more demanding with regard to subject content. *It is particularly interesting in this connection that the work in music, for which specialist teaching, including peripatetic teaching[1], is most common, is the area of the curriculum in which the work of the able, average and least able children is most evenly matched to their abilities[2]. It is also striking that classes in schools where the holders of posts of special responsibility have marked influence were much more successful than others in matching the work to the abilities of all children, including the most able.[3]* Furthermore, the better match that is achieved in the basic skills may well occur because all the students who intended to teach in primary schools are given some training in the teaching of these skills, because carefully graded materials are available, and because dealing with children who find it difficult to learn to read is another common area of specialisation in primary education.

Some children in inner city schools

8.36 In recent years efforts have been made to provide for the special needs of some children in inner city schools. In the survey, inner city schools generally had a more favourable staffing ratio than similar schools in 'other urban' areas, and in some of these schools resources were noticeably better than average.[4]

8.37 Some of the schools in inner city areas contained a larger proportion than most of children whose home language was not English, and also of those children from some indigenous families who find it difficult to gain as much as they should from their schooling.[5] While both the HMI survey and the NFER tests indicate that standards of performance are lower than average in these schools, neither can show whether the efforts made in recant years have improved the levels of performance. *The survey indicates that children in inner city schools are more likely than others to be under-estimated by their teachers and least likely to be given work which extends their capabilities. This strongly suggests that further improvement in the children's performance is possible.[6]*

---

[1] Chapter 3 iii, paragraphs 12–14
[2] Chapter 6 ii, Tables 30–32.
[3] Chapter 7 vi, Note 12
[4] Chapter 7 ii, paragraphs 4 and 5
[5] Chapter 2 iv, paragraph 22
[6] Chapter 7 ii, paragraphs 11–13

8.38 *Further study is required of how improvements may be brought about. Some research has already been undertaken in this field but more is necessary in primary schools, particularly to identify conditions that are likely to be effective in teaching children from these areas.*

8.39 *The need to raise teachers' assumptions about children's capabilities has special relevance here. It may also be that in these schools, with a preponderance of children who find learning difficult, special care should be taken to support and encourage those children who make average or good progress, not least in order that they should set a standard of work at which others may aim. This may require yet more teachers and resources. The slower children still need painstaking and thorough attention if they are to reach minimum standards of literacy and numeracy; and children who come to school with little or no English cannot be expected to make progress in school unless, as a result of careful teaching, they achieve a sufficient command of English, which is for them a foreign language.[1]*

iii. CLASS AND SPECIALIST TEACHING

8.40 Even when the curriculum is clearly defined and priorities are agreed upon, the range of work and the range of pupils present a formidable challenge to the knowledge and skill of an individual teacher. The older and the more able the children, the more obvious this difficulty is for the individual teacher. This is made plain by the present inclination in many schools to rely on one or two teachers for the teaching of music or French, and the poor showing of some subjects, including science and craft, which are commonly the responsibility of the class teacher. *A fuller use of teachers' particular strengths could make a useful contribution to the solution of this problem.*

8.41 *The traditional view has been that the one class to one teacher system should be maintained for nearly all of the work to be done. The class/ teacher system has a number of potential advantages: the teacher can get to know the children well and to know their strengths and weaknesses; the one teacher concerned can readily adjust the daily programme to suit special circumstances; it is simpler for one teacher than for a group of teachers to ensure that the various parts of the curriculum are coordinated and also to reinforce work done in one part of the curriculum with work*

---

[1] Chapter 2 iv

done in another. These advantages are not always exploited, as is shown particularly in the case of mathematics.[1] *Nevertheless potentially, and often in practice, these are important advantages and care should be taken to retain and use them.*

8.42 *They are not overriding advantages in all cases. When a teacher is unable to deal satisfactorily with an important aspect of the curriculum, other ways of making this provision have to be found. If a teacher is only a little unsure, advice and guidance from a specialist, probably another member of staff, may be enough. In other cases, more often with older than with younger children, and much more often in junior than in infant schools, it may be necessary for the specialist to teach either the whole class or a group of children for particular topics. In some cases, specialists may have to take full responsibility for the teaching of a class or classes other than their own in an area of the curriculum such as music, where expertise is short; perhaps more subjects, in particular science, should be added to the current list, at least for the older children.*

8.43 A danger of specialist teaching is that the work done by a specialist may be too isolated from the rest of the children's programme, and this needs to be guarded against by thorough consultation between teachers. *The teacher responsible for the class may be the best placed to coordinate the whole programme of the class. Care needs to be taken to ensure that the programme of the specialist's own class is not too fragmented, and is arranged to utilise the complementary strengths of other teachers.* This may require more than a simple exchange of teachers between two classes. If specialist teaching is taken too far, the timetable becomes over-complex and does not allow variations in the arrangements which circumstances may require from time to time.

8.44 Some schools already adopt forms of cooperative or team teaching which allow teachers to work from their strengths. These arrangements can work well if areas of responsibility are clearly designated, though teams are rarely large enough to permit full coverage of the curriculum using the particular interests and abilities of teachers. No blanket solution is being suggested here. *The critical points are: can class teachers manage to provide all that is necessary for particular classes? If not, what must be done to help them to manage satisfactorily and in a way that is, on balance, advantageous?*

---

[1] Chapter 5 i and iii

Posts of special responsibility

8.45 It is disappointing to find that the great majority of teachers with posts of special responsibility have little influence at present on the work of other teachers.[1] *Consideration needs to be given to improving their standing, which is the product of the ways in which the teachers with special posts regard themselves and also of the attitudes that other teachers have towards them.*

8.46 *It is important that teachers with special responsibility for, say, mathematics should, in consultation with the head, other members of staff and teachers in neighbouring schools, draw up the scheme of work to be implemented in the school; give guidance and support to other members of staff; assist in teaching mathematics to other classes when necessary; and be responsible for the procurement, within the funds made available, of the necessary resources for teaching the subject. They should develop acceptable means of assessing the effectiveness of the guidance and resources they provide, and this may involve visiting other classes in the school to see the work in progress.[2]*

8.47 *Teachers holding posts of responsibility require time to perform their duties, some of which must be carried out while the school is in session;* they also need to keep up to date with current knowledge and practices elsewhere, and this may take time outside normal school hours. The role of heads is rarely discussed specifically in this report because of the way in which the survey was arranged. In average sized and large schools the minor part of heads' time is usually spent in teaching, but this part is of considerable importance and should be safeguarded.

The deployment of teachers in medium and large schools

8.48 *In schools of medium or large size, perhaps where the staff is eight or more strong, it may be possible to provide the necessary range and level of specialisation from within the staff, especially if this requirement is taken into account when teaching appointments are made.*

8.49 Practice in the vast majority of schools, primary and secondary, makes it plain that criteria additional to class size are taken into account when deploying staff. Arrangements that are made either for freeing a

---

[1] Chapter 4 i, paragraph 5
[2] Chapter 7 vi

teacher from teaching, or for enabling a teacher to teach groups smaller than a whole class, have the effect of increasing the size of the basic class unit; this is so whether small groups are withdrawn for special teaching or whether two teachers temporarily share the teaching of a class in one teaching area.

8.50 Considerations other than class size which are taken into account when deploying staff are: the ages and special needs of children; the expertise of individual teachers; and the need for teachers, especially the head, to undertake, in addition to teaching duties, administrative responsibilities and liaison on behalf of the school. *It is a matter of judgement in individual cases precisely how the criteria are balanced and how duties are allocated, but the survey evidence suggests that some shift in the deployment of teachers is worth considering.*

8.51 *After detailed analysis, the survey data led to the conclusion that differences in class sizes in classes of between about 25 and about 35 children made no difference to the children's scores on the NFER objective tests, or to the closeness of the match of the work to the children's abilities[1], or to the likelihood that a wide range of common items would be included in the curriculum.[2] On the other hand, classes of these sizes performed worse in certain ways if they contained mixed rather than single age groups[3]: the 7 and 11 year olds were more likely to be given work that was too easy; the 9 and 11 year olds scored less well on the NFER tests. This is probably because, for children of these ages and in classes of these sizes, the teacher's perception of the class as a whole masks the considerable differences between the children and especially the differences in their rates of progress. It is probably unreasonable to expect most teachers to work as effectively with mixed age classes of about 30 children as they would with single age classes of that size. Class size is only one factor to be taken into account when determining suitable staffing standards. The findings of this survey do not mean that staffing standards could safely be tightened, but rather that there are some ways of using teachers' time, including those described in the next paragraph, which could bring bigger benefits than simply minimising class sizes.*

8.52 *Bearing in mind what has been said in the previous paragraph about class sizes and about classes with mixed age groups, heads and teachers*

---

[1] Chapter 7 iv, paragraphs 17 and 18. The statements in this sentence also apply to class sizes of less than 25, many of which had a mixture of age groups and were in rural areas, and also to classes of more than 35

[2] Chapter 6 i, paragraph 5

[3] Chapter 7 iv, paragraph 20

could usefully consider how staff might be deployed in order to make the best uses of the strengths of individual teachers, to employ holders of posts of responsibility[1] most effectively and to allow some time for the preparation of work. In large and some medium sized schools it might, within limits, be worth arranging for one or more teachers additional to the head to be free of full responsibility for a class, though in virtually full-time teaching contact with children. This would make registered class sizes larger than they would otherwise be, given the number of teachers. On different occasions these teachers could be used to teach their own specialism and to enable teachers with other curricular responsibilities to be freed to assess the extent to which modifications are needed in the programme of work in their subject; they, or the teachers they free, might be able to assist others in the course of their teaching; work with sub-divisions of a class in order to meet the specific needs of individuals or groups of children; or undertake the teaching of other classes, particularly in areas of the curriculum where expertise is short. In schools of medium size, these arrangements may be possible only if staffing standards are particularly generous, except in so far as the head uses his own teaching timetable for these purposes.

Special responsibilities and small schools

8.53 *In small schools the number of teachers on the staff is likely to be too small to provide the necessary specialist knowledge in all parts of the curriculum. The teachers in a group of schools can profitably share their skills in planning programmes of work and a number of small schools (and large) have benefited from doing so as a result of their own enterprise, under the guidance of local authority advisers, through teachers' centres or with the help of Schools Council and other curricular projects.[2]*

8.54 *Teachers in some small schools already make arrangements to exchange classes, for example for half a day a week during the summer term or from time to time. Some local authorities employ visiting teachers of sufficient status to be accepted as specialists by teachers, including heads, of the schools they visit. They are most commonly involved in remedial education and music, but in a few areas a range of specialist advice is provided and the visiting teacher works alongside the class teacher. This is a practice that might usefully be extended and avoids the danger, for*

---

[1] Chapter 7 vi
[2] Chapter 4 iii, paragraph 11

which there is some tentative evidence in the survey, that peripatetic teaching directed solely at special groups of children, whether the most able in music or the least able in reading, has little carry over effect on the levels of work for the rest of the children.

iv THE PROFESSIONAL DEVELOPMENT OF TEACHERS

8.55 *Teaching primary school children is a difficult and complex task, and teachers cannot be expected to master all they need in one short burst of training. Initial training must be followed throughout a teacher's career by a supporting pattern of in-service education and training.* In-service training is partly given through attendance at specially designed courses, but also takes place within a school through observing others at work and through discussion with fellow teachers and particularly the head, teacher trainers, teachers' centre wardens, visiting advisers and inspectors, and others.

The curricular range expected of individual teachers

8.56 *The survey confirms that it is necessary that all primary school teachers should be trained to teach children to read, write and do mathematics; courses should enable teachers to understand the nature of these skills and how to teach them in a context which relates to the rest of school work and to the real world in which children live. Intending primary school teachers should be helped to recognise the importance of teaching children to observe carefully, encouraging them to try to explain what they have noticed, and to test their explanations.[1] Constructional activities associated with the careful observation of natural and man-made objects can provide a useful link in helping children to develop an attitude of scientific enquiry. Teachers should acquire a sound, even if restricted, range of practical skills in science as well as in art and crafts which they can build upon during their years of teaching[2].*

8.57 *Students preparing to teach in primary schools require opportunities to exploit their academic strengths and to convert them in ways that will enable them to contribute in a specialist sense in a primary school. This*

---

[1] Chapter 5 i
[2] Chapter 5 iv and v

presupposes the ability to initiate and implement programmes of work in the teacher's own area of expertise and to advise and help other teachers who may have different strengths.

The assessment of pupils' needs

8.58 *It is vital that teachers should be knowledgeable in what they teach; it is just as necessary that they should be able to assess the performance of their pupils in terms of what they next need to be taught.* The survey has shown that even some experienced teachers find it difficult to judge the appropriate level of work[1]. Yet, if this is not done, the children's application to their work and their rate of progress may suffer. Without doubt, a lack of application can result in disorder and this, though fortunately rare, was certainly associated with a poor match between children's work and their capacity, and also with low scores in NFER tests[2].

8.59 *This suggests that a vital part of initial and in-service training should be directed towards helping teachers to assess children's capabilities and to establishing a sufficiently high, but reasonable, expectation of what the children are capable of achieving. Familiarity with telling examples of work done by children of different ages and abilities is an aid to this. Knowledge of commercially produced diagnostic tests (and, to a lesser extent, standardised tests) can also help, though these generally cover only a limited part of the curriculum. Initial training in these matters will certainly need to be supplemented after the teacher is qualified.*

Teaching methods

8.60 Limiting teaching to a form that relies on posing questions, or allowing children to pose questions, and then leaving them to ferret out the answers seems to be less effective than a more controlled form of teaching with explanations provided step by step. But a combination of the two approaches was consistently associated with slightly better scores in the NFER tests and with the best match between tasks to be done and the children's ability to undertake them.[3]

---

[1] Chapter 6 ii
[2] Chapter 7 v, paragraph 28
[3] Chapter 7 v, paragraphs 25–27

8.61 If one method of teaching were plainly superior it would be simpler to know what to provide in initial and in-service training. *What the survey indicates is that teachers need to become familiar with a range of teaching techniques, to understand the advantages and disadvantages that each has, and to choose what is best for their immediate purpose[1]. One factor to be taken into account when making a choice is the teacher's own strengths and interests. Strengths and weaknesses are often reflected by the children's reactions and by how well they learn. Careful assessment of the children's progress has implications for the teacher's approach, too. It is not sensible for teachers to attempt to use a teaching technique that is clearly beyond their operational skill and is therefore inefficient; neither is it right to be satisfied with one's present range if it is clear that too little learning on the part of the children is taking place.*

The training of teachers holding posts of responsibility

8.62 Teachers may act in an advisory capacity for an area of the curriculum, or for some facet of schooling such as assessment, or in connection with the education of pupils with special needs. *When they are ready to undertake further responsibility of this kind much needs to be done through in-service training, which may require secondment, to help them to carry out their functions and to extend expertise in their main field.*

8.63 New teachers may sometimes be able to participate in an advisory way with regard to an area of the curriculum, though usually teachers are more ready to act in this way when they have had some years' experience and have developed confidence and skill.

8.64 *Teachers in posts of special responsibility[2] need to keep up-to-date in their knowledge of their subject; to be familiar with its main concepts, with the sub-divisions of the subject material and how they relate to one another. They have to know enough of available teaching materials and teaching approaches to make and advise upon choices that suit local circumstances. And they should be aware of the ways in which children learn and of any sequences of learning that need to be taken into account. Additionally, these teachers should learn how to lead groups of teachers and to help others to teach material which is appropriate to the abilities*

---

[1] Chapter 3 v
[2] Chapter 4 i

of the children. They should learn how to establish a programme of work in cooperation with other members of staff and how to judge whether it is being operated successfully. They should also learn how to make the best use of the strengths of teachers of all ages and to help them to develop so that they may take on more responsibility. Particular care should be taken to foster the special qualities of intuitive and gifted teachers. Heads need, in consultation with those concerned, to make quite clear the responsibilities of individual teachers.

Some aims for in-service training

8.65 *The survey points to two major functions for in-service education, in both of which the teachers in individual schools have a major part to play. The first is to arrange for positive staff development, based on the strengths of individuals. This should lead to extending the influence of experienced and able teachers.[1] The second is to raise the expectations which teachers have of children and, in doing so, to achieve a clearer definition of the curriculum. Additionally, the nurturing of teachers who have a particular ability or who are willing to increase their expertise in those parts of the curriculum where there is general weakness, like science and craft, may be the surest way to make advances in these fields.* Despite efforts by the Nuffield Foundation and the Schools Council, work in science is weak[2]; a slow but steady build up from the points of strength of individual teachers is probably the only sure way forward.

v. LOOKING FORWARD

8.66 This survey could not have been conducted without the goodwill and cooperation of the teachers; in giving this they exhibited the same characteristics that have led to the establishment of good and friendly relations among themselves and with the children they teach[3]. In that teaching, they show their concern for individuals, and a positive determination to help children acquire the basic skills of literacy and numeracy[4]. During years when the public at large has seemed to be critical of schools the relations between teachers and individual parents have become closer

---

[1] Chapter 7 vi, Note 12
[2] Chapter 5 iv
[3] Chapter 5 i
[4] Chapter 5 ii and iii

and more friendly; and the curriculum has broadened to include much that is of value. Good relations within the schools, increasingly good relations with parents, and a thorough concern for teaching the basic skills are solid foundations on which to build further.[1]

8.67 Taking primary schools as a whole, the curriculum is probably wide enough to serve current educational needs. But the demands of society seem likely to continue to rise; literacy and numeracy will no doubt remain matters of great interest but priorities may well change within these areas and in other parts of the curriculum. The immediate aim, especially for the average and more able pupils, should probably be to take what is done to greater depth rather than to introduce content that is new to primary education. To do this it is important to make full use, on behalf of schools as a whole, of teachers' strengths and to build on the existing knowledge of individual teachers without losing the advantages that are associated with the class teacher system.

8.68 However the requirements of society come to be formulated, teachers have the main responsibility for responding to them; but they do not have the sole responsibility. Teacher trainers, including teachers' centre wardens, and also advisers, inspectors and others in professional contact with schools all have a part to play, as do administrators with responsibility for distributing resources among schools. The public must will the means as well as make demands and parents, as the evidence backing the Plowden Report[2] shows, have a special role.

8.69 Given support from all these sources, a survey of primary education in the 1980s should be able to report that today's strengths have been maintained and steady progress made in the exacting task of educating young children.

---

[1] Chapter 3 iv
[2] *Children and their primary schools.* HMSO, 1967

Appendices

APPENDIX A   THE FEASIBILITY AND PILOT SURVEYS

The feasibility survey

1 Following wide consultation throughout HM Inspectorate and under the direction of a central steering committee, schedules of questions for HMI survey teams, and questionnaires for teachers of classes to be inspected and heads of schools to be involved were prepared.

2 In November 1974 teams of two HMIs visited four schools, each of which contained 7, 9 and 11 year old teaching groups. In each school HMI inspected selected classes and jointly agreed their assessments. Teachers in the schools completed questionnaires.

3 In the light of this study the general method to be adopted was confirmed.

The pilot survey

4 In the Spring Term 1975 a full pilot study covering 56 schools was carried out. These schools were chosen to cover as wide a range as possible.

Table .A1   The types of school covered in the pilot survey

Category	Description
1.	Urban; 3-form entry
2.	Urban; 2- or 1-form entry
3.	Suburban; 2-form entry
4.	Suburban; 1-form entry
5.	Rural; number on roll 200 or more
6.	Rural; number on roll 100 or less
7.	Special features that might affect the arrangements to be adopted

Note: Schools with open plan buildings, a handicapped class or nursery class were included in Category 7

5 As a result of the pilot and feasibility surveys alterations to administrative arrangements and questionnaires were made where appropriate. The survey design assumed a class teacher with responsibility for a class. For

the main survey the class teacher's questionnaire was restricted to questions which could be taken to describe the organisational context of a group of children of a particular age within the class. A question on social class which had a high refusal rate in the pilot survey was deleted. The staffing section of the heads' questionnaire was presented as a separate document and the HMI schedules were also carefully revised.

APPENDIX B   THE SAMPLE DESIGN: A TECHNICAL ACCOUNT

Summary notes

6 The sample was drawn in three stages.

Stage 1: the first stage units were schools. These were stratified by HMI Division (8), organisational type (infant, junior, junior with infants, first and first with middle) and three size bands (≤ 1, 2 and ≥ 3 form entry). For first and middle schools all schools of two form entry or larger were grouped together. In addition certain strata were empty. Total strata: 95. Stratification by form entry was approximate, using the number of 8, or in the case of infant schools, 7 year olds as a measure of size. Selection of schools was made with a probability proportional to form of entry (pps); this procedure yielded an overall sampling fraction of 2.6 per cent and a sample of 542 schools.

Stage 2: the second stage units were teaching groups. Within each of the 7, 9 and 11 year old age groups a teaching group was selected at random. Where there was only one teaching group selection was automatic.

Stage 3: this stage was carried out only for the purposes of administering the NFER tests. It applied to the 9 and 11 year old age groups only. The sampling units were individual children. Where a teaching group contained 21 or more children a systematic sample, with a 50 per cent sampling fraction, was taken. Where there were 20 or fewer in the teaching group all children were selected.

The sample of schools and teaching groups (Stages 1 and 2)

7 The survey design called for samples of 7, 9 and 11 year old teaching groups. Not all types of school in the survey included all of these age

groups (although self-evidently every school included at least one of the age groups). Where any of the specified age groups occurred in a school it was always included in the sample.

8 To draw these samples directly it would have been necessary to have details of the number of children of different ages in every individual class in maintained primary schools. The Department does not hold information in this detail and so the two stage sample was drawn.

Stratification

9 Before the first stage selection, schools were stratified according to HMI Division, organisational type and a 'measure of size' relating to the expected number of teaching groups per age group.

10 Stratification by HMI Division ensured an even geographical spread for the sample. Although the Inspectorate in England is centrally organised most inspectors are territorially based. For administrative purposes they were divided into 8 divisions (since reduced to 7). It was decided, as a general rule, to draw the HMI teams for sampled schools in a division from the divisional complement of inspectors; thus stratification by division was convenient administratively. Although the divisions vary considerably in the number of schools they cover, the divisional complements reflect this; thus the same sampling fraction could be used in each division without causing disproportionate survey work loads. However, to minimise any possible regional bias HMI also carried out inspections in divisions other than their own.

11 School organisation types are defined by the age range they cover. Thus the organisational type of a school dictated which of the three survey age groups would be present, see Table B1.

Table B1 The relationship between school organisational type and the survey age groups

Age groups	School type				
	Infant	First	Junior	Junior with infant	First and middle
7	Yes	Yes	No	Yes	Yes
9	No	Possible	Yes	Yes	Yes
11	No	No	Yes	Yes	Yes

12 Stratification by school type ensured that the sampling fraction was the same at each age group. The only difficulty was with first schools; some covered 9 year olds, some did not. The sample was drawn using lists relating to the position at January 1974. At this time there were 1,787 first schools of which 1,044 covered 9 year olds, ie 58 per cent of the total of all first schools. In the sample 61 per cent of first schools (28 out of 46), covered 9 year olds, so the sample accurately reflected the national picture.

Equal probability selection of teaching groups

13 The main focus of the survey was on teaching groups rather than schools. The sample design thus needed to yield an equal probability sample of teaching groups at each age. There were two possible ways of achieving this. Either one or all the teaching groups in each age group in each school could have been included in the survey. It was decided to employ the former approach since:

(a) this would allow the available manpower to cover the number of schools necessary, given the objectives of the survey,

(b) inspecting several groups across a number of schools would yield more statistically useful information than considering the same number of groups in one school,

(c) this would permit the teaching group sample sizes to be controlled and would allow the time needed to survey a school to be standardised, with consequent administrative benefits.

14 To achieve an exact equal probability sample of teaching groups it was necessary to know the numbers of teaching groups at each age in each school. As pointed out above (paragraph 8) such detailed information was not available. Therefore single age class organisation was assumed and the form entry (ie the number of classes per age group) was estimated using the number of 8 year olds (7 year olds in infant schools) as a measure of size.

Table B2 Stratification of schools into form entry strata using the number of 8 year olds as a measure of size

Strata	Number of 8 year olds
One-form entry or less	35 or less
Two-form entry	36 to 80
Three-form entry	81 or more

Note: A few schools in the three-form entry stratum had in excess of 120 8 year old children and were therefore probably four-form entry. There were too few such schools to justify another stratum.

7 or 8 year olds were used since they were in the middle of the primary age range. Appropriate arrangements for weighting, to adjust any imbalance caused by the use of a measure of size, are described in Appendix D.

15 Because of the small number of first and middle schools the 2- and 3-form entry strata for these schools were collapsed. The number of strata in the design was 112, (8 regions × 5 school types × 3 categories of form entry=120—8 due to collapsing of 2- and 3-form entry strata for middle schools; total 112). Several regions did not have first or first and middle schools; some did not have one form entry infant schools. This gave 17 empty strata so that the sample was actually covered by 95 strata. The number of schools in some of the strata, particularly in the stratum for one form entry schools, was small and where the sampling fraction did not yield an exact number of schools the last school selected for the sample was included or excluded on a probability basis. Because of this the number of schools in the one form entry stratum was slightly higher than expected (120 instead of 116).

Table B3 The design and actual sampling fraction for schools

Schools	1-form entry	2-form entry	3-form entry	All
Population number	8,032	8,582	4,140	20,754
Sample number	120	245	177	542
% Sample—actual	1.49	2.86	4.28	2.61
design	1.43	2.86	4.29	2.58

16 Schools were sampled with a sampling fraction proportional to the form entry, so as to give an approximate, equal probability sample of

teaching groups at each of the three survey ages. The sampling fractions for schools are given in Table B3. The minor discrepancies apparent between actual and design percentages of the sample are due at one form entry to sampling error (discussed above); and at 3 form entry to rounding error.

17 The design sampling fraction for teaching groups was 1.43 per cent at each age group. The higher sampling fractions at 2- and 3-form entry are cancelled out by the larger number of teaching groups. The fact that some schools did not cover all three age groups did not affect this sampling fraction.

18 Because the stratification by a measure of size was approximate, it was possible that the effective sampling fractions at each age group would differ from the design figure. However, the effective sampling fractions were very close to the design fractions.

Table B4 The design and actual sampling fractions for teaching groups in percentages

	7 year olds	9 year olds	11 year olds
Design	1.43	1.43	1.43
Actual	1.20	1.26	1.23

The adjustment was calculated as follows:

Define m_i , the number of teaching groups according to the sample design in each of the form entry strata, $i = 1, 2, 3,$

m'_i , the actual sample sizes, $i = 1, 2, 3$

n_{ij} , the number of teaching groups in the jth school of the ith stratum, $i = 1, 2, 3, j = 1, 2, \ldots m_i$.

By definition

$$m'_i = \frac{1}{i} \sum_j n_{ij} \ , \ i = 1, 2, 3 \ .$$

133

Consider the 2-form entry stratum:

The effective sampling fraction $= \dfrac{m_2}{2m'_2} \cdot 2f$

$$= \dfrac{m_2}{m'_2} \cdot f$$

The same result holds for the 1- and 3-form entry strata, the effective sampling fractions being

$$\dfrac{m_1}{m'_1} \cdot f \text{ and } \dfrac{m_3}{m'_3} \cdot f$$

Adjusting for the differences in strata size gives the overall sampling fraction as

Overall sampling fraction =

$$\left(\dfrac{m'_1}{m'_1+m'_2+m'_3} \cdot \dfrac{m_1}{m'_1} + \dfrac{m'_2}{m'_1+m'_2+m'_3} \cdot \dfrac{m_2}{m'_2} + \dfrac{m'_3}{m'_1+m'_2+m'_3} \cdot \dfrac{m_3}{m'_3} \right) \cdot f$$

Rewriting $(m_1+m_2+m_3)$ as m, the design sample size,
and $(m'_1+m'_2+m'_3)$ the actual sample size, as m'
and simplifying gives

$$\text{Overall sampling fraction} = \dfrac{m}{m'} \cdot f \cdot$$

In other words, the actual sampling fraction is the design sampling fraction multiplied by the ratio of the design to the actual sample size.

Sampling for objective NFER tests (Stage 3)

19 Part of the survey involved giving objective tests to the children. These tests were supplied by the National Foundation for Educational Research (NFER), who also arranged their administration by teachers, and did preliminary analysis of the results. Tests were administered to 9 and 11 year old age groups (details are given in Appendix I).

20 In the main survey, tests were given towards the end of the summer term of the academic year in which the school was inspected. In order to establish satisfactory administrative procedures the tests were also given during the pilot survey at the time of HMI's visit.

21 A third stage in the sample was required because it was decided, in consultation with the Department of Education and Science, to use the test data as coming from a sample of individual children (see Appendix I). The third stage was drawn as follows: where a 9 or 11 year old teaching group inspected by HMI had fewer than 21 children they were all tested. Otherwise alternate children in the teaching group were tested, using the class register to take the sample. This reduced the variation in the number of children per teaching group tested (ie cluster size). It also avoided unnecessarily large samples. It was known that the sample design would tend to undersample teaching groups in vertically grouped schools. This would, of course, be corrected by reweighting (see Appendix D). However, these teaching groups in vertically grouped classes were liable to be small; the differential sampling of children introduced further weighting which tended to counterbalance the existing weights, thus moving the sample of children nearer to being a sample in which all children had an equal chance of appearing.

APPENDIX C ADMINISTRATION

22 It was decided that HM Inspectorate could provide sufficient manpower, within the context of their normal commitments, to inspect classes in about 540 schools in England over a period of five terms beginning in the Autumn Term 1975. This was judged sufficient, working on estimates of the likely sampling errors, to give a reasonable overall national picture, but it would not allow regional or other analyses requiring comparisons of small sub-divisions of the sample.

23 Before the start of each term a group of sample schools was nominated for inclusion in that term's programme. This group had approximately the correct proportion of schools from each division and as far as possible it reflected the characteristics of the full sample regarding the number of different types of schools. Thus the load in each division was roughly constant throughout the survey and the sample schools were covered in a balanced way. This allowed valid interim analyses to be carried out.

24 A programme of inspections for the term was organised for each division. The amount of time needed was fixed as shown in Table C1.

Table C1 Time allowed for inspection of schools according to type and size

Type of school	Age group covered	Time (days)
Infant	7	$1\frac{1}{2}$
Small junior with infant	7, 9 and 11	2
1-form entry junior with infant	7, 9 and 11 ⎫	
2/3-form entry junior	9 and 11 ⎬	$2\frac{1}{2}$
2/3-form junior with infant	7, 9 and 11 ⎭	3

Note: i. First schools were allocated between $1\frac{1}{2}$ and $2\frac{1}{2}$ days depending on their size and whether they contained 9 year olds.

ii. Combined first and middle schools were treated as junior with infant schools.

iii. In all cases $\frac{1}{2}$ day was allowed additionally for discussion.

25 Local Education authorities were informed before the start of each term which of their schools would be affected. The head of each survey school was notified by letter of the coming visit a few weeks before it was due to take place. He or she was given the proposed date and requested to complete a table giving details of each class in the school. (The letter and table are reproduced in Annex A.)

26 One member of each HMI survey team, termed the visiting inspector, was responsible for the conduct of the survey in each school. At least three weeks before the inspection was due to take place the visiting inspector paid a preliminary visit to the school to explain the purpose of the survey; the fact that schools would not be reported on individually was stressed.

27 A further purpose of the preliminary visit was to select the teaching groups to be involved in the survey. This was done as follows: the table completed by the head showed which of the three survey age groups were to be found in the school. Disregarding any special units or classes, any entries of 6 or more children in the 7, 9 or 11 year columns represented a survey teaching group (for circumstances in which groups of less than 6 children were acceptable, see Appendix F para 3). For each of the three age groups where there was only one teaching group this was automatically selected. Otherwise one teaching group was selected at random for each age group. One of the schedules provided for the survey team included an alphabet devised to assist randomisation. On one twenty-sixth of forms the alphabet started at A and went through to Z; on the next twenty-sixth it started at B and went through Z to end at A; and so on. Before distribution to survey teams the forms were shuffled, to ensure that they were used in random order. The classes of a given age group from which one

was to be selected for the purposes of the survey, were listed according to the alphabetical order of the surnames of their class teachers. The first name to appear alphabetically in the given alphabet on the HMI schedule indicated the class to be chosen.

28 The final purpose of the preliminary visit was to distribute and discuss the questionnaires to be completed by the head and the teachers from whose classes teaching groups had been selected for the purpose of the survey. The teachers concerned were asked to complete the forms and return them to the visiting inspector before the main survey visit. This enabled the visiting inspector to ensure that the forms were fully completed. (The three questionnaires are reproduced in Annex A.)

29 If a student teacher was due to take a survey class at the time of the inspection it was left to the discretion of the head whether the student was replaced by the permanent class teacher for the duration of the survey. It was made clear that students, like teachers, were not being assessed. In fact it was very rare indeed for students not to be replaced. In all cases class teachers, not students, were required to fill in the class teacher's questionnaire.

30 Following the feasibility study at least one and often both of the pair of HMI inspecting classes for the main survey had had previous experience in the survey. Both HMI inspected each of the relevant classes and made agreed returns. The pairs of HMI were rearranged for each inspection. Although the majority of inspections carried out by an HMI were in schools in his or her home division, inspections in other parts of the country were also undertaken. The majority of HMI in the survey team had taught in primary schools and all had had experience of inspecting primary schools. Some subject specialists whose main teaching experience had been in secondary schools were brought into the survey team each term. These arrangements were made to reduce, as far as possible, the results of any individual bias.

31 The first analyses of returns were made by groups of HMI each containing at least one primary specialist and relevant subject specialists.

APPENDIX D WEIGHTING AND THE CALCULATION OF STANDARD ERRORS

Weighting

32 The estimates calculated from the sample were weighted to take account of difference in selection probabilities. In the case of schools the differences were part of the design; with teaching groups the differences arose when the number of teaching groups predicted by the measure of size was different from the number actually found.

Note : Define c_k , the expected number of teaching groups according to the measure of size (i.e the form entry), $k = 1, 2, 3,$

a_{gk} , the actual number of teaching groups for age group g in school k,

$g = 7, 9, 11,$
$k = 1, 2, \ldots m.$

Then

School weight $= 1/c_k$,

Teaching group weight $= a_{gk}/c_k$.

33 The sampling fraction was defined in terms of schools. Therefore, for school-based estimates, the sample is self-weighting by region. However because the proportions of 1-, 2- and 3-form entry schools varied slightly between divisions the sampling fraction for teaching groups also varied marginally, lying between 1.41 and 1.51 per cent. In view of the evaluative nature of much of the HMI survey data, and the size of the sampling errors, these differences were of no consequence and, for simplicity, teaching group estimates were calculated on the assumption that the sample was self-weighting by region. The argument did not hold when calculating the estimates for objective test (NFER) survey data. The data were objective and accuracy was of paramount importance in view of the very small sampling errors. Therefore the divisional samples were weighted for the purposes of dealing with objective test (NFER) survey data.

138

Standard errors for HMI survey data

34 Weighting affects the calculation of standard errors. A slightly biased estimate of the variance of a proportion can be deduced as shown in the following note, ignoring the finite population correction.

Note: Take a sample, size n, from an infinite population.

Define $\quad d_i \quad = 1 \qquad$ if the characteristic of interest is present for the ith sample member,

$$= 0 \qquad \text{otherwise,}$$
$$i = 1, 2, \ldots n.$$

p , the population proportion of interest.

Then $\quad \hat{p} \quad = \displaystyle\sum^{n} \frac{d_i}{n}$.

$$\mathrm{var}\,(\hat{p}) \quad = \mathrm{var}\left(\sum^{n} \frac{d_i}{n}\right) \,,$$

$$= \frac{1}{n^2}\,(n\,\mathrm{var}\,(d_i)) \quad, \qquad \text{since the } d_i \text{ can be treated as independent,}$$

$$= \frac{1}{n}\,(\hat{p}\,(1-p)^2 + \hat{q}\,(\hat{p})^2) \quad,$$

$$= \frac{1}{n'^2}\sum^{n} w_i^2\,\mathrm{var}\,(d_i) \quad,$$

$$= \frac{1}{n'^2}\sum^{n} w_i^2\,\hat{p}\,\hat{q} \qquad ,$$

$$= \frac{\overset{n}{\Sigma w_i^2}}{n'} \cdot \frac{\hat{p}\ q}{n'}\ .$$

Thus the variance, taking account of the weights, has a factor $\dfrac{\overset{n}{\Sigma w_i^2}}{n'}$ compared to the estimate using the weighted sample size but ignoring the weights.

Taking the case of weighted school-based estimates we have:

```
Sample size = n   =  540
            n'  =  300
            w_i =  1        119 cases
                =  0.5      244 cases
                =  0.33     177 cases
```

This gives a factor of 0.66. In other words, assuming an unweighted sample with sample size n' we overestimate the variance by a factor of 1.5. The standard error is overestimated by a factor of 1.2.

35 The actual design involved stratification, so that the estimate based on a simple random sample size n will actually be slightly more of an overestimate than indicated. The factor will vary when estimates are drawn from part of the sample. Therefore, for simplicity, all standard errors for school-based estimates were calculated assuming simple random sampling and reduced by an arbitrary 10 per cent; this procedure erred on the side of caution.

36 The 7 year olds required slightly more weighting and the 11 year olds slightly less than the 9 year olds. The percentage of groups with a weight of one was 57 and 68 per cent respectively. The variance estimate, treating the sample as if it were a simple random sample and using the weighted total, is 80 per cent of the weighted value for 9-year-old teaching groups. The standard error is 87 per cent. Thus, again using an arbitrary value, all standard errors for 7, 9 and 11 year olds were increased by 10 per cent.

Table D1 The weights applied to the 9 year old teaching groups

Weights	1	2	3	4	1/2	3/2	5/2	1/3	2/3	4/3	5/3	Total before weights	Total after weights	% with weight of 1
Number of teaching groups	240	27	4	2	25	35	1	1	12	24	2	373	424	64

37 The calculation of standard errors for the child-based estimates presented in Chapter 6 iii (see Annex I for more details) was not straight-forward. The sample design was three stage, with unequal and non-proportional selection probabilities for unequal size clusters (the teaching groups). The methods of calculating the standard errors for this sample design are not known and therefore simplifying assumptions had to be made.

38 The teaching groups were assumed to have come from a stratified random sample. This assumption is true for teaching groups in the one form entry stratum, but it ignores the school clustering in the 2- and 3-form entry strata. The assumption implies that two or more teaching groups of the same age could be selected from the same school. In fact, this could not happen but, even under the assumption, with a sampling fraction for groups of about one in 70 in the 2- and 3-form entry strata the chances of more than one teaching group of the same age being selected from a particular school are extremely slight. Therefore the assumption seems reasonable.

39 The design was thus reduced, under the assumption, to two stages. From Kendall and Stuart[1] it seemed that the second stage variation could be ignored. Of course where the whole teaching group was selected there was no second stage variance.

40 With these two assumptions, the design was reduced to a stratified random sample of unequal clusters with unequal and non-proportional selection probabilities. Even here an approximate method for the calculation of standard errors had to be employed.

41 Regardless of the approach to the calculation of the standard errors the mean had to be estimated by a ratio estimate, which is biased. The actual form of the estimate used did depend upon the assumptions made for the calculation of the standard errors. It can be shown that the bias of the mean is negligible and that the approximation for the standard errors is satis-factory. The formulae used are presented below. They are taken from Kish.[2]

References:

[1] Kendall and Stuart. *The advanced theory of statistics* Vol. 3 Section 39.46.

[2] Kish L. *Survey sampling* John Wiley 1965 Chapter 6.

Define n_{kl} ,   the number of teaching groups (clusters) in the stratum with form entry k in region l, $k=1, 2, 3, l=1, 2, \ldots 8$

m_{jkl} ,   the number of children in the jth teaching group sample for the stratum with form entry k in region l, $j=1, 2, \ldots n_k, k=1, 2, 3, l=1, 2, \ldots 8$

y_{ijkl} ,   the score for the ith child in the jth teaching group sample in the stratum with form entry k in region l, $i=1, 2, \ldots m_{jkl}, j=1, 2, \ldots n_{kl}, k=1, 2, 3, l=1, 2, \ldots 8$

δ_{jkl} ,   a weight of 1 or 2 depending whether $m_{jkl} \leqslant 20$ or $m_{jkl} > 20$

t_{jkl} ,   the number of teaching groups in the jklth school

f_{kl} ,   the expected number of teaching groups (the form entry) for the klth stratum

r_l ,   the sampling fraction for the lth region.

Set $a_{jkl} = \delta_{jkl}\, t_{jkl}\, r_l\, y \cdot_{jkl}/f_{kl}$

         $b_{jkl} = \delta_{jkl}\, t_{jkl}\, r_l\, m_{jkl}\,/f_{kl}$.

Then
$$y = \frac{\sum_j \sum_k \sum_l a_{jkl}}{\sum_j \sum_k \sum_l b_{jkl}} = \frac{a_{ooo}}{b_{ooo}} \, ,$$

$$\mathrm{Var}\,(\bar{y}) = \frac{1}{b^2_{ooo}} \left[\sum_k \sum_l (l - r_l) \left\{ \mathrm{var}\,(a_{kl}) + \bar{y}^2 \mathrm{var}\,(b_{kl}) - 2\bar{y}\, \mathrm{cov}\,(a_{kl}b_{kl}) \right\} \right].$$

Where var $(a_{kl}) = \dfrac{n_{kl}}{n_{kl}-1} \left\{ \dfrac{\sum\limits_{j} a_{jkl} - (\sum\limits_{j} a_{jkl})^2}{n_{kl}} \right\}$

var $(b_{kl}) = \dfrac{n_{kl}}{n_{kl}-1} \left\{ \dfrac{\sum\limits_{j} b_{jkl} - (\sum\limits_{j} b_{jkl})^2}{n_{kl}} \right\}$

cov $(a_{kl} b_{kl}) = \dfrac{n_{kj}}{n_{kl}-1} \left\{ \dfrac{\sum\limits_{j} a_{jkl} b_{jkl} - \sum\limits_{j} a_{jkl} \sum\limits_{j} b_{jkl}}{n_{kl}} \right\}$

The ratio mean is of the form y/x, where, in our case, x is the sample size. The bias occurs because x is a random variable. We have

$$\text{Bias } (\bar{y}) = -\rho_{\bar{y}x} \, c_x \, \delta_{\bar{y}}$$

Where

$\rho_{\bar{y}x}$ is the correlation between the mean and the sample size

c_x is the coefficient of variation of x,

$\delta_{\bar{y}}$ is the standard error of the mean.

Thus

$$\begin{aligned}
\text{Bias } (\bar{y}) \quad &\leqslant c_x \, \sigma_{\bar{y}} \\
&\leqslant 0{\cdot}01 \times 70{\cdot}33 \\
&\leqslant 0{\cdot}006
\end{aligned}$$

The correlation $\rho_{\bar{y}x}$ is likely to be very small. Hence any bias in the ratio mean can be safely ignored. This agrees with the conclusion of Kish. He also demonstrates that with $c_x < 0{\cdot}1$ the bias in the variance estimate is likely to be between 3 and 6 per cent, which is negligible. Clearly, with $c_x = 0{\cdot}017$, any bias can be safely ignored.

APPENDIX E WITHDRAWAL AND REPLACEMENT OF SCHOOLS AND RESPONSE RATES

Withdrawal and replacement of schools

42 When the original sample was drawn, at the first stage one or two extra schools were randomly selected in each stratum to provide replacements if any sample schools had to be withdrawn. A total of 21 schools were withdrawn and replaced. Reasons for which schools were withdrawn and replaced are given in Table E1.

Table E1 Reasons for which schools were withdrawn and replaced

Reason for withdrawal	Number of schools withdrawn & replaced
Closed subsequent to selection	5
Major change of type	5
Recently inspected or surveyed (including 2 schools from the national primary survey feasibility and pilot studies)	6
Serious illness of headteacher	3
Exceptional local circumstances	2

43 The first two categories shown reflect the time lag between selection and the survey visit for many schools. The category 'major change of type' included change to a middle school (which took the school outside the survey coverage) : the amalgamation of two schools (one of which was in the sample) : or the splitting of a survey school into two separate schools.

44 A number of schools, although they changed type, were not withdrawn and replaced. The overall effect of such changes on the sample was small. This was because the main change from design to actual sample was due to the formation from infant schools of new first schools, and the majority of these did not cover the 9 year old age group by the time of the inspection.

Table E2 The design and actual sample of schools by type

	Infant	Junior	Junior with infant	First	First with middle	Total
Design sample	146	141	202	46	7	542
Actual sample	136	136	202	59	9	542

Response rates

45 *HMI survey data.* HMI gathered data on all the 542 schools in the sample. Data for one school were lost in the post. Another school had such a flexible organisation that the categories of class teacher and teaching group did not apply. The survey data for this school did not accurately reflect the true situation and it was therefore excluded. Neither school was replaced. Both schools were junior with infant. The sample estimation procedures were adjusted to take account of the loss, which was too small to have any noticeable biasing effect. The response rates for data collected by HMI are shown in Table E3.

Table E3 The response rates for HMI survey data

	Schools	7-year-old teaching group	9-year-old teaching group	11-year-old teaching group
Design total	542	406	376	347
Actual total	540	404	373	344
% response	99.6	99.5	99.2	99.1

Notes: 1. The design totals take account of the school type changes shown in Table E2.
2. The number of 9-year-old classes and the number of 11-year-old classes inspected were both one less than the design total because one junior with infant school, by chance, had no 9 year olds and one junior school had an age range of 7–10 years.

46 *Objective test (NFER) survey data.* All the schools involved in giving objective (NFER) tests supplied data. In three cases the BD and NS6 reading tests were accidentally reversed and given to the wrong age group. Data from these schools were excluded. Further, in some cases a few children of the wrong age were tested and they were also excluded.

Table E4 The response rates for objective test (NFER) survey data and reasons for which children were withdrawn

Test	Age group	Children tested	Children withdrawn because:		% Response
			a. Error in admin. of tests	b. Wrong age	
BD Reading Test	9	5289	46	78	97.7
NS6 Reading Test	11	5083	41	87	97.5
E2 Mathematics Test	11	5072	–	80	98.4

47 The incidence of unusable responses was too small to be of any significance. Estimates were made, when the sample was designed, of the likely sample sizes for these tests. No data on teaching group organisation were then available, so single age class organisation had to be assumed. This meant that the sample sizes were over-estimated. The estimates were 5,750 and 5,400 at 9 years and 11 years old respectively. The achieved sample sizes seem reasonable and are close enough to the estimates, which were known to be over-estimates, to suggest there was little likelihood that significant numbers of children who should have been tested were omitted, for whatever reason.

48 *Summary of response rates for HMI and objective test (NFER) survey data.* The two schools for which no data existed in the HMI survey data are included in the objective test (NFER) survey data: the three schools for which no data existed in the objective test (NFER) survey data are included in the HMI survey data.

Table E5 The design and actual sample of teaching groups in relation to the collection of HMI and objective test (NFER) survey data

	Design sample	Actual sample: HMI survey data	Actual sample: objective test (NFER) survey data	Total actual sample
7 yr	406	404	–	–
9 yr	376	373	372	370
11 yr	347	344	343	341

See footnote 2 to Table E3

APPENDIX F   A COMPARISON OF SURVEY SAMPLE AND NATIONAL ESTIMATES

49 By comparing survey sample estimates with other data it is possible to check whether the sample is truly representative or whether it is biased. The survey fieldwork was spread over five terms and inevitably during that time there were changes both in the population and the sample. Thus any comparison must be approximate.

50 Two comparisons were made. First, the survey sample and national distributions of schools by organisational type were compared. The stratification of schools by type was affected slightly by the factors

mentioned in the previous paragraph. However, the sample was found to reflect the national population very closely. The national figures were estimated using a weighted average with weights of 0.6 and 0.4, to take account of the fact that three-fifths of the sample schools were covered in the academic year 1975/76.

Table F1 A comparison of the national* and survey sample distribution of schools by type in percentage

Type of school	Maintained schools in England		Weighted average for the 2 years	Actual sample distribution	Difference (sample— average)
	January 1976	January 1977			
Infant	20.7	20.2	20.5	19.3	(−1.2)
Junior	19.1	18.8	19.0	19.3	(+0.3)
JMI	48.5	46.8	47.8	49.0	(+1.2)
First	10.2	12.3	11.0	10.5	(−0.5)
First and middle	1.5	1.8	1.6	2.0	(+0.4)
Total	100.0	100.0	100.0	100.0	—

* Source: *Statistics of Education*, Volume 1, 1976 and 1977. HMSO

51 The second check on the sample was to estimate the total number of children in each of the three survey age groups and to compare these estimates with the actual figures. The sample was not designed to give these estimates; they were only calculated for this check. In order to avoid observing extremely small groups of children, or even individuals, the minimum size for a teaching group was set at six children (except in the rare cases where the total number of children in an age group in any class was less than six). Thus the sample estimates of the number of children in each age group were biased upwards. (This bias does not, of course, affect the data given in the report.)

52 The numbers of children aged 6, 8 and 10 at 31 August 1975 and 31 August 1976 were used to estimate the actual national totals. As before a weighted average was formed.

53 The actual standard errors for the sample estimates would be difficult to calculate, but approximate calculations, taking account of the work carried out in relation to objective test (NFER) data, suggest that they were about 2 per cent of the total. Thus a 95 per cent confidence interval for each sample estimate was about ±4 per cent of the estimate. Taking account of the upward bias due to the definition of a teaching group, which is likely to

be small, and the marginal discrepancies shown in Table F1, the comparison in Table F2 indicates that the sample was otherwise representative. In fact, it can be concluded with some confidence that the sample was not biased in any way.

Table F2   The number of children in the 7, 9 and 11 year old age groups as estimated from the sample and calculated from published statistics[1]

Age group	Numbers (1,000) calculated from official statistics	Sample estimates (1,000)	% difference (sample—official)
7 year olds	707.9	701.9	(−0.8)
9 year olds[2]	672.5	690.2	(+2.6)
11 year olds[2]	620.7	658.6	(+6.1)

[1] *Statistics of education*, Volume 1. 1976 and 1977
[2] The 9 year and 11 year old figures exclude children in middle schools

APPENDIX G   METHODS OF ANALYSIS

54 The calculation of standard errors for descriptive statistics has already been discussed in Appendix D.

55 This appendix describes how associations in the data were examined and includes examples of some analyses.

Hypothesis testing

56 Strict attention was paid to the logic of hypothesis testing. As far as possible hypotheses were generated without reference to the data. As is usual with a survey of this kind some hypotheses were generated as the analysis proceeded. In only a few cases, for example where differences between classes in different types, sizes and localities of school were examined, were the data systematically searched for 'significant' differences.

Significance testing

57 Significance testing was extensively used, but bearing in mind the way that hypotheses were constructed associations were not necessarily

excluded if they did not show significance. It should be noted that weighting of data affects significance tests, but the effects are not known.

58 Where the concern was only with establishing associations within the sample it was legitimate to use the data unweighted. Where the concern was to establish associations between population estimates weighting was necessary. For class-based data the weighted data were tested. It was assumed that weighting would not affect significance levels too much (see Appendix D for details of weighting) but even so the levels were used cautiously. For school-based data it was possible to compare unweighted data separately by the size of school as determined by forms of entry. Provided the pattern was the same for all three sizes the data were then amalgamated and handled unweighted for both sample and population associations. Otherwise reporting was done separately by size of school.

Techniques used

59 For nominal and ordinal data, analysis was by tabulation, using the chi-squared significance tests.

60 For the test scores from the NFER, one-way analysis of variance was used with associated Tukey and Scheffé tests.

61 A difficulty with this analysis was that the mean scores were derived from samples of children of different sizes. The sample size ranged from 3 to 25, but 83 per cent of the samples fell inside the range 11 to 20 children.

62 The mean scores were analysed without weighting by the sample sizes since the majority of sample sizes were so close. The effect will be to make the analysis more sensitive to random fluctuations in the mean scores, hence the procedure was conservative.

Reading Scores over time: weighted least squares regression

63 The formula used for this regression is given below. It was taken from Draper and Smith.[1]

---

[1] Draper and Smith. *Applied regression analysis.* John Wiley & Son

$$b = \frac{\sum_i w_i x_i y_i}{\sum_i w_i x_i^2}$$

where $w_i = \dfrac{1}{\sigma^2_i}$ σ^2_i being the variance of the mean.

This gave an R^2 of 0·92.

An analysis of the partition of the sum of squares is given in Table G1.

Table G1 Analysis of partition of sum of squares for weighted regression

Source of Variation	Sum of squares	Degrees of freedom	Mean square	F ratio
Regression ($b \sum w_i x_i y_i$)	20.78	1	20.78	21.99**
About regression	1.89	2	0.95	
Total ($\sum w_i y_i^2$)	22.67	3		

Clearly the regression does explain a very high proportion of the variance. An unweighted regression, which involves making the clearly unreasonable assumption that the four variances are equal, produced an R^2 of only 0.75.

Widely taught items

64 In Chapter 5 there is a description of an analysis in which the proportion of classes undertaking a range of widely taught items was calculated. The items were considered in subject groupings, as combinations of subjects, and as a whole.

65 The data were searched and any item which occurred in 80 per cent or more of the classes in an age group was noted. In some cases, eg art and history, the requirement was that the class should be undertaking at least one item from a given range. This allowed for the greater, quite legitimate, diversity in these areas. For history and geography the 9-year-old classes did not quite meet the 80 per cent limit.[1] This was only important in that it affected the consistency of definition of the group of items. The percentages of classes undertaking the items (75 and 76 per cent respectively) were so near to 80 per cent that the discrepancy was considered unimportant.

[1] Chapter 6 i

66 Science does not feature because no item was undertaken by 80 per cent or more of classes at any age. Multiple choice items, as for history and art, were developed but the range of these items was so wide as to be meaningless.

67 A calculation was made of the proportion of classes undertaking work relating to all the widely taught items in each subject.[1] As is to be expected, because of the larger number of items involved, the proportion of classes satisfying the group of language items is a little lower than the others. Again, to be able to interpret the results it is necessary to be sure that there were not a greater than expected number of classes which satisfied all but one aspect of the group of widely taught items. This indeed did not happen, see Table G2. For instance, for the items in mathematics at 11 years, by chance, we would expect to get percentages of 6, 30 and 53 compared to the actual percentages of 12, 23 and 65.

68 By chance, we would expect to have 18, 11 and 13 per cent of the 7, 9 and 11 year old classes undertaking work in relation to all items in each subject, assuming the groups of items in each subject were not associated.

69 The probability was calculated, under the hypothesis that the groups of widely taught items in each subject were not associated in any way, of obtaining the actually observed percentages of classes undertaking work relating to all items, namely 29, 19 and 24 per cent of 7, 9 and 11 year olds respectively.

70 The method used was (for 11 year olds):
i. Probability of a class undertaking all widely taught items in all four subjects assuming independence

$$= 0.65 \times 0.57 \times 0.58 \times 0.61$$
$$= 0.13$$

ii. Probability of 81 or more of the 344 classes undertaking all widely taught items in four subjects, assuming independence (ie 24 per cent or more) using the normal approximation to the binomial gives:

$$Z_c = \frac{|81 - 45| - 0.5}{\sqrt{(344 \times 0.13 \times 0.87)}}$$
$$= 5.7$$

Probability $= 0$, to 4 decimal places

---

[1] See Annex to Chapter 6, Table 28

Table G2 The distribution of classes by the number of groups of items taught in relation to each subject

	Percentage of classes satisfying							Total %	Total classes
	0 aspect	1 aspect	2 aspects	3 aspects	4 aspects	5 aspects	6 aspects		
Language									
7 year olds	−	*	1	7	13	25	54	100	404
9 year olds	−	*	3	9	15	30	43	100	373
11 year olds	*	1	3	5	15	23	53	100	344
Mathematics									
7 year olds	35	65	X	X	X	X	X	100	404
9 year olds	24	76	X	X	X	X	X	100	373
11 year olds	18	25	58	X	X	X	X	100	344
Aesthetics									
7 year olds	1	5	22	73	X	X	X	100	404
9 year olds	2	11	23	63	X	X	X	100	373
11 year olds	2	10	31	58	X	X	X	100	344
Social Abilities									
7 year olds	5	30	65	X	X	X	X	100	404
9 year olds	1	6	18	29	46	X	X	100	373
11 year olds	1	2	10	26	61	X	X	100	344

*=less than 0.5%
X=not possible
Note: An 'aspect' is a number of similar items within a subject from those listed in Chapter 6 i, paragraph 5, grouped together for the purpose of this analysis.

153

The probabilities for 7 and 9 year old classes are also 0 to 4 decimal places. Obviously the model used is approximate, since it is assumed that all classes could undertake all items, whereas in practice the maximum figure would be 57 per cent. However, the approximation is clearly reasonable.

Match Assessments

71 In order to assess the overall match achieved by a class a 'match rating' was calculated. To do this each of the 11 match questions was recoded as shown:

		Usual code	New code
Considerable over expectation		5	1
Slight over expectation	reasonably	4	2
Good match	satisfactory	3	3
Slight under expectation	match	2	2
Considerable under expectation		1	1

72 This recoding was done separately for each ability group. Adding the recoded match questions makes sense, since the higher the code the better the match. In practice virtually no over expectation was recorded, so a low match rating almost always implies under-expectation.

APPENDIX H   DEFINITION OF LOCALITY

73 The sample was not stratified by locality because no definitions of particular schools by locality could reliably be made prior to HMI visits. HM Inspectors defined schools by locality at the time of the inspection; this information was subsequently employed in the analysis of the findings.

74 The following definitions were used:

Inner city: the centre of large conurbations and the inner rings of large cities.

Rural: hamlets, villages and small towns with a population of 15,000 or less.

'Other urban': any area not able to be categorised as inner city or rural, including towns with populations exceeding 15,000 and certain parts of cities and conurbations.

APPENDIX I   ATTAINMENTS IN READING AND MATHEMATICS (NFER)

75 In parallel with the national primary survey carried out by HMI the Department of Education and Science contracted the National Foundation for Educational Research (NFER) to administer and to conduct preliminary analyses of the results of objective tests in reading and mathematics; these are considered here. This information is referred to as the NFER data, although the further analyses and interpretation of the data and the conclusions reached are the responsibility of the Department. The data are intended to contribute to a balanced view of work in primary schools. They also constitute, in part, the latest stage of the national survey of standards in reading at 11 years. The overall results of these tests will not be fully comparable with the results of the Assessment of Performance Unit's

monitoring programme from 1978 onwards. However, it should be possible to establish some links between scores from the tests and those from APU monitoring of performance in reading and mathematics at age 11 years.

i. THE PUPIL SAMPLE

76 The children who were tested were drawn at random from the 9 year and 11 year old teaching groups surveyed by HMI. The mathematics test used was derived from items suitable for 11 year olds produced in the Tests of Attainment in Mathematics in Schools Project. The selection of pupils from within the teaching groups, rather than from the whole year group within each school, was necessary to ensure that the data could be related to HMI's assessments, which were made in terms of teaching groups. The results presented in this chapter are, however, representative of all 9 year olds and all 11 year olds in primary schools in England.

77 The data were analysed in terms of performance of individual pupils. Where a teaching group contained 20 children or fewer the test was given to every pupil; otherwise every second child was tested. This procedure avoided testing an unnecessarily large sample and offered some statistical advantages (see Appendix G). Average scores for all pupils tested in each teaching group were also calculated, so that NFER scores and HMI assessments could be directly related (see Chapter 7).

78 The selection of children from teaching groups, although essential for this survey, provided a possible source of error because the national primary survey excluded children in permanent classes with a special function, for example, full time remedial classes. However, it was estimated on the basis of the class organisation tables completed by heads that only 0.5 per cent of children were in such classes. Even if they had been tested and every child had scored zero the overall national mean scores would have been depressed by only minimal amounts: for example in the case of the 11 year old reading scores by 0.2. The possible effect is so small that it can safely be ignored.

79 A second possible source of bias concerns streaming. If too many high or low stream classes had been included in the survey, the ability of the sample children would not accurately have reflected the national level of ability. The greatest care was taken to ensure that selection of teaching groups was random. Streaming occurred in only 12 of the 9 year old teach-

ing groups and 13 of the 11 year old teaching groups and there was a mixture of high and low stream classes in each case; it is therefore unlikely to have been a major factor. Nevertheless to test for bias arising from streaming the test results were recalculated, excluding all children in streamed classes, and there was no significant change in the national mean scores. For instance the mean score of the NS6 reading test was reduced by 0.15. The influence of streaming on the sample can confidently be discounted.

80 In order to ensure that administrative procedures were effective a selection of test materials was used alongside the HMI pilot survey in the spring term 1975.

81 The complete tests were given to approximately equal numbers of children in June 1976 and June 1977, in each case to children in the groups nspected during that particular academic year but not at the time of the inspection visits.

ii. THE TESTS

Reading Test NS6 (National Survey Form Six)

82 This test was used to assess the reading performance of 11 year olds. It is of the sentence completion type, in which the child has to choose the appropriate missing word from a given selection, and in which items are progressively more difficult. It was decided for a number of reasons that the NS6 was the appropriate test to use. The Bullock Report (1975) recommended that, pending the introduction of a new national monitoring system, currently being developed by the Assessment of Performance Unit of the Department of Education and Science, 'The NS6 (reading) test should remain in operation'[1]. NS6 was used in earlier surveys of reading standards carried out in 1955, 1960 and 1970, and so, since the surveys were similarly designed, direct comparison is possible between present and previous findings. In all, the test contains 60 items. It has consistently been shown to have a very high degree of reliability (0.95). It was suggested in the 1970/1 report[2] that two items in the test had become more difficult for children because they contain words which have become outdated. How-

---

[1] *A language for life.* Para 3.8 HMSO 1975.
[2] *The trend of reading standards.* K B Start and B K Wells. NFER 1972

ever, subsequent to the 1970 survey, unpublished research carried out by NFER showed that the items in question retained the same 'facility value' as before and that they were reasonably correctly positioned within the test. Results of the present survey support these findings.

Reading Test BD

83 Like NS6 this is a traditional, norm referenced test and was devised by NFER. The test contains 44 items. It was used to assess the reading performance of 9 year olds. Since reading standards at 9 years of age had not previously been monitored nationally the matter of comparability did not arise. BD was chosen because it was reliable and suitable for the age range in question; further, it was standardised relatively recently in 1969.

Mathematics Test E2

84 This test was used to assess the mathematical performance of 11 year olds. Since mathematical standards at 11 years of age had not previously been measured nationally it was not possible to select a test comparable with others used earlier for similar purposes. E2 was specially compiled for the survey from test items constructed by NFER in connection with the Tests of Attainment in Mathematics in Schools project[1]; they were chosen as being suitable for 11 year olds. The test could be employed in future surveys to make comparisons of standards. The test comprises five sets of items; geometry, graphical representations, handling everyday situations, properties of whole numbers and a group of eight items covering additional aspects of mathematics. A total raw score has been calculated based on all 50 items.

iii. QUALITY OF DATA AND COMPARISONS WITH PREVIOUS SURVEYS

Level of response

85 In any survey the response rate has an important influence on the

---

[1] Similar test material is being used in the work undertaken for the DES Assessment of Performance Unit

quality of the data. The higher the response rate, the more reliable is the information which is obtained. In the present survey all schools initially responded; but owing to errors in school administration the data from three schools had to be excluded, thus the response level was 99 per cent. This is an exceptionally high rate of response.

Age correction

86 Age adjustments have been made to all the NFER data so that all scores relate to a fixed age chosen as the mean age of the sample. The advantage of this is that it allows valid comparisons to be made between groups or individuals within the sample. If age adjustments were not made, older children would have an advantage over younger ones in any comparison since it is well established that in the primary age range test performance is directly associated with age.

87 Samples from different surveys tend to have different mean ages. Accordingly, in order to make comparisons over time, it is sometimes necessary to restandardise some data at an age other than the sample mean. In this report, though the changes were small, the survey data have been restandardised as necessary to ensure that valid comparisons can be made with past data. The ages to which test results have been standardised are shown alongside the test results tables.

Standard errors

88 Mean scores are presented in the tables accompanied by their standard errors; these indicate the limits within which the sample means are likely to have deviated from the means which would have been obtained if the whole population had been tested. The larger the standard errors, the less statistically precise the results. If the standard error is multiplied by 1.96 a 95 per cent confidence interval is obtained. That is to say, if the survey was repeated many times, on average in 19 times out of 20 the confidence interval surrounding the sample mean would include the true, fixed mean of the whole population to whom the test might have been given.

Comparisons with previous surveys

89 Before any comparisons can be made with the results of previous surveys using Reading Test NS6, the quality of the data from all of the

surveys has to be considered. In each survey random sampling was used. The information used here about the earlier surveys is based on *The trend of reading standards* (Start and Wells, NFER, 1972). There seemed to be no difficulty in comparing the 1960 and 1976/7 results. Certain factors have to be taken into account before comparing the 1976/7 results with those obtained in 1955 and 1970.

90 The 1955 sample was drawn at random to be representative of Wales as well as of England. The way in which the survey was designed does not permit sample estimates for England only to be abstracted. However, in 1960 reliable parallel national surveys of Wales and England were carried out for 11 year olds; no significant differences were found between the performance of the Welsh and English children. It is therefore reasonable to assume, particularly since the 1955 school population of Wales was about one-fifteenth of that of England, that the inclusion of Wales in the earlier survey did not significantly bias the result.

91 One difficulty regarding the 1970 survey lies in the low response rate, which was 73 per cent. One in four schools did not provide data partly because of a postal strike, and partly for other undertermined reasons. If the schools which did not provide data were different in any way from those which did take part, the test results would have been biased. The size and direction of the distortion, if it exists, cannot be measured. Particular caution also has to be exercised in using the mean score of the 1970 survey because of the large standard error attached to it.

92 In order to establish the trend in reading standards since 1955, the findings of the four surveys were compared, see Table I1. In the present survey 4,955 children, age corrected to 11 years 2 months, took the NS6 test in 343 schools. A mean score for all pupils of 31.13 out of a possible 60 with a standard error of 0.33 was obtained.

93 Middle schools, deemed primary, were not in existence in 1960, and there were only 21 such schools by 1970. The 1976/7 survey did not cover middle, deemed primary, schools and therefore its coverage is slightly different from that of the earlier surveys. However, there is no reason to suppose the performance of 9 and 11 year olds in middle schools would be different from that of children of the same age in other types of primary schools. Moreover, there were only 1,153 middle schools out of a total of 21,371 primary schools in January 1976. Thus the exclusion of these schools in the 1976/7 survey would not be likely to affect the comparisons made.

iv. PRESENT STANDARDS AND TRENDS

Reading standards of 11 year olds

Table I1 NS6 Reading Test results from national surveys of samples of pupils in primary schools in England age corrected to 11 years 2 months. (See Graph 1)

	Date of survey 1955[1]	1960	1970	1976/1977
Mean score	28.71	29.48	29.38	31.13
Standard error	0.55	0.52	0.92	0.33
Number of schools covered	na	na	69	343
Number of children tested	na	na	1470	4955
Response rate (%)	na	na	73	99

na : not available. Special schools excluded.

[1] This survey covered England and Wales. An under-estimate of the England only mean in the region of 0.06 is possible.
[2] There is a total of 60 items in this test.

Graph 1. NS6 Reading Test: Mean scores from national surveys with 95% confidence intervals mean age: 11 years 2 months

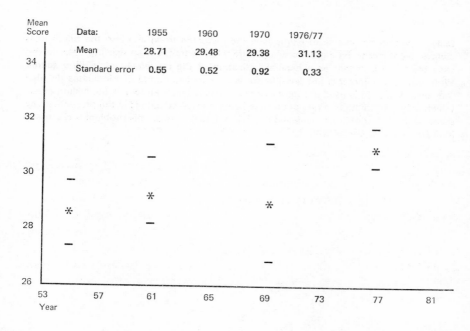

Data:	1955	1960	1970	1976/77
Mean	28.71	29.48	29.38	31.13
Standard error	0.55	0.52	0.92	0.33

94 It can be said with confidence that the data from the four surveys were consistent with a rising trend in reading standards between 1955 and 1976/77. (See Graph 2, NS6 reading test; mean scores for national surveys.)

Graph 2. NS6 Reading Test: Mean Score for National Surveys. Mean age: 11 years 2 months.

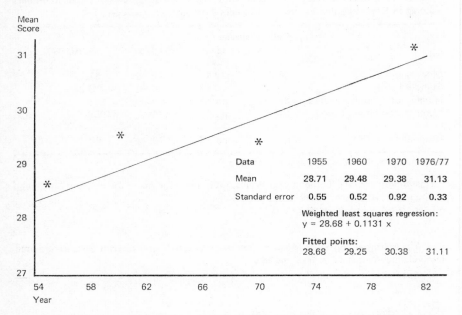

Data	1955	1960	1970	1976/77
Mean	28.71	29.48	29.38	31.13
Standard error	0.55	0.52	0.92	0.33

Weighted least squares regression:
$y = 28.68 + 0.1131 \, x$

Fitted points:
28.68 29.25 30.38 31.11

Note: It would be unwise to extrapolate the indicated trend line into the future. It is always necessary to be cautious when extrapolating trends from existing data. In this case the trend is meant as a general indication of the movement of reading scores. With only four points it is not possible to be sure that the trend line indicates detailed movements. If NS6 is used in future there is a special factor known as the ceiling effect which may lead to the true rate of any rise being under-estimated; in the present survey some of the ablest children achieved nearly maximum scores. This problem is discussed in *A language for life* (HMSO 1975), paragraphs 2.31 to 2.34.

Reading stardards of 9 year olds

Table I2 BD Reading Test. Mean score for a sample of pupils in primary schools in England age corrected to 9 years 2.6 months

Number of schools involved	Number of children tested	Mean score	Standard error
372	5,165	20.13	0.24

There is a total of 44 items in this test

95 Five thousand one hundred and sixty-five children (age corrected to 9 years and 2.6 months), in 372 schools took the BD reading test. A mean score was obtained of 20.13, with a standard error of 0.24.

96 Since this test had not previously been given to a nationally representative sample of 9 year olds, comparison with previous standards cannot be made.

Standards in mathematics of 11 year olds

Table I3 E2 Mathematics Test. Mean scores for a sample of pupils in primary schools, age corrected to 11 years 2.5 months

Number of schools involved	Number of children tested	Mean Raw score
346	4,991	27.97
Standard error		0.30
Scale		

97 A total of 4,991 children (age corrected to 11 years and 2.5 months) in 346 schools took the E2 mathematics test. A mean total raw score was obtained of 27.97 with a standard error of 0.30. Some comments on the educational implications of the results are made in Chapter 6 iii, paragraphs 29 to 32. Examples of the items used are given at the end of this appendix.

v. DIFFERENCES BETWEEN BOYS AND GIRLS

Table 14 NS6 Reading Test. Mean scores for a sample of boys and girls in primary schools in England, age corrected to 11 years 2.5 months

	Number of schools involved	Number of children tested	Mean score	Standard error
Boys	341	2493	31.55	0.39
Girls	339	2462	31.10	0.36
All pupils	343	4955	31.32	0.33

Note: In this table the corrected age used is the mean age for the sample
There is a total of 60 items in this test

98 It can be seen from the standard errors associated with each mean that the difference was not statistically significant.

Table 15 NS6 Reading Test. Percentile distribution for boys and girls and all pupils at age 11 years 2.5 months
Possible range of scores 0–60

Percentile	Boys' score	Girls' score	Boys' score minus girls' score	All pupils
90	47.0	45.8	(+1.2)	46.3
80	42.4	41.6	(+0.8)	42.1
70	38.8	37.9	(+0.9)	38.4
60	35.3	34.7	(+0.6)	35.0
50	32.4	31.0	(+0.5)	32.2
40	29.0	28.4	(+0.5)	28.8
30	25.0	24.2	(+0.8)	24.6
20	20.4	20.3	(+0.1)	20.3
10	14.3	15.0	(−0.7)	14.6

99 The percentile figures in the table may be interpreted as follows: the percentile of 90 indicates that 90 per cent of the boys scored 47.0 or less and 10 per cent scored more; the percentile of 20 indicates that 20 per cent of boys scored 20.4 or less and 80 per cent scored more.

Table 16 BD Reading Test. Mean scores for a sample of boys and girls in primary schools in England, age corrected to 9 years 2.6 months

	Number of schools involved	Number of children tested	Mean score	Standard error
Boys	370	2610	19.56	0.29
Girls	366	2555	20.72	0.28
All pupils	372	5165	20.13	0.24

Table 17 BD Reading Test. Percentile distribution for boys, girls and all pupils age corrected to 9 years 2.6 months
Possible range of scores 0–44

Percentile	Boys' score	Girls' score	Boys' performance compared with girls	All pupils
90	32.9	32.5	(+0.4)	32.7
80	28.5	28.6	(−0.1)	28.5
70	25.0	25.6	(−0.6)	25.2
60	21.9	23.0	(−1.1)	22.5
50	19.2	20.7	(−1.5)	20.0
40	16.6	18.5	(−1.9)	17.5
30	13.5	15.4	(−1.9)	14.4
20	10.6	12.6	(−2.0)	11.5
10	7.2	8.9	(−1.7)	8.0

See paragraph 99 of this appendix for an interpretation of this table

100 The girls obtained a higher mean score in reading test BD than the boys, this difference is statistically significant, although, for practical purposes, very slight. It is of interest that despite the overall lower scores of boys the top 10 per cent of boys marginally outscored the top 10 per cent of girls.

Table 18 E2 Mathematics Test. Mean scores for a sample of boys and girls in primary schools in England, age corrected to 11 years 2.5 months

MEAN	Number of schools involved	Number of children tested	Mean raw score
Boys	345	2515	28.30
Girls	343	2476	27.64
All pupils	346	4991	27.97
STANDARD ERROR			
Boys			0.35
Girls			0.32
All pupils			0.30

There are 50 items in this test

Table 19 E2 Mathematics Test. Total raw score. Percentile distribution for boys, girls and all pupils, age corrected to 11 years 2.5 months

Possible range of scores 0–50

Percentile	Boys' score	Girls' score	Boys' score minus girls' score	All pupils
90	41.8	40.2	(+1.6)	41.0
80	37.8	36.5	(+1.3)	37.1
70	34.4	33.3	(+1.1)	33.9
60	31.5	30.5	(+1.0)	31.0
50	28.4	27.9	(+0.5)	28.2
40	25.6	25.1	(+0.5)	25.4
30	22.9	22.4	(+0.5)	22.7
20	19.4	19.3	(+0.1)	19.3
10	14.6	14.8	(−0.2)	14.7

See paragraph 99 for an interpretation of this table

101 It can be seen that as the level of scoring increases the slight superiority of boys over girls also increases. There was no statistically significant difference in the total scores achieved by boys and girls.

vi. MATHEMATICS TEST E2

102 Most of the items used in this test are to be included in future surveys and so cannot be made public. Those reproduced on pp 167 to 171 have been chosen to indicate the range of items. They include some on which children scored well and others that many found too difficult. The percentage of children getting each item right is shown to the right of the test. The children were generally allowed 45 minutes to complete the test, but longer it they were still making progress through it.

A.

Ann   Bob   Carol David Eric Fred

Each time somebody buys a   savings stamp for 10p they
stick a square on the chart.

		Percentage of correct responses
a.	Who has saved most?	94
b.	How much money have the children saved altogether?	84

B.

How much change would you expect from a £1 note
if you spent 43p?   83

167

	Percentage of correct responses

C

This 4 centimetre square
has been cut into 5 pieces

A,B,C,D and E

The shape of D is a square.

Which two pieces can be fitted together to make a square?

_____ and _____   92

D

1p   2p   5p   10p   50p

I have these coins in my purse.
Put a ring around the sums below which I can pay exactly.

8p   2p   54p   66p   69p   59

E

Paddington	06 15	07 50	09 45	10 45	11 45	12 45
Reading	06 55	08 24	10 19		12 19	
Swindon	07 38	09 08	10 54	11 19	13 04	13 19
Bath	08 14	09 44	11 29	12 18	13 42	14 22
Bristol	08 30	10 00	11 45	12 35	14 00	14 40

This is part of the railway timetable, showing the times of trains
leaving Paddington and the times they leave stations on the way to
Bristol.

Use the information from the timetable to answer this question:

Which is the latest train which I could take from Reading to be
in Bath by 2 o'clock in the afternoon?

_____   47

168

F. The cost of a week's shopping					Percentage of correct responses

	Mrs Jones	Mrs Smith	Mrs Brown	Mrs Green
Groceries	£10.00	£7.50	£5.50	£8.20
Bread	£ 1.50	£0.72	£0.85	£1.20
Meat	£ 3.53	£2.75	£2.65	£3.25

How much does Mrs Brown spend altogether on a week's shopping?

_____   64

G.

$$16 \times 35 = 560$$

$$so \ 17 \times 35 = 560 \ + \ \Box$$

Underline the number for which ☐ stands

A. 560   C.   17

B.   35   D.   16   37

H.   * * * is a 3 figure number

Tick the true statements

A.   * * * must be bigger than 99

B.   * * * must be bigger than 100

C.   * * * must be smaller than 999

D.   * * * must be smaller than 1000

E.   * * * must be bigger than 199   20

I.   Which of these has the smallest answer

A.   5673 x 8

B.   5673 ÷ 8

C.   5673 − 8

D.   5673 + 8   _____   61

J.   7 hundreds, 5 tens and 12 units total   _____   69

		Percentage of correct responses
K	Which fraction is smallest? Put a ring around the smallest fraction $\frac{1}{2}$ $\frac{3}{4}$ $\frac{3}{8}$ $\frac{1}{4}$ $\frac{5}{8}$	<u>40</u>
L	A class has between 20 and 30 children. When they have teams of 6 there are no children left over. When they have teams of 5 one team is one short. How many children are there in the class? _____	<u>49</u>
M	 This graph can help you to convert miles to kilometres, or kilometres to miles. Use the graph to convert 1.6 kilometres to miles.	<u>28</u>

170

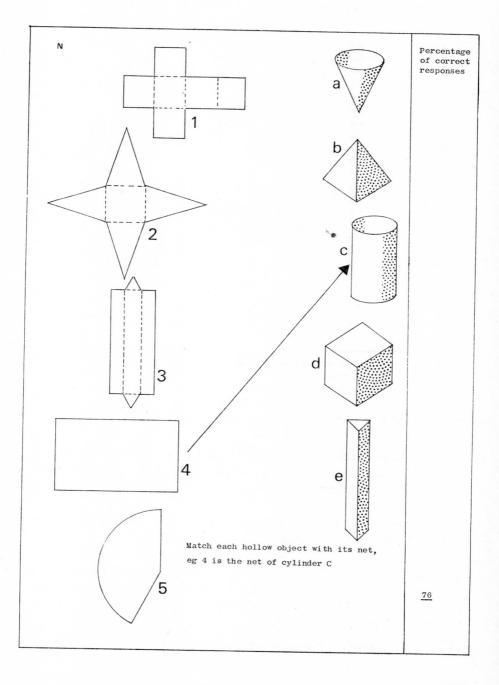

N

1

a

b

2

c

3

d

4

e

5

Match each hollow object with its net,
eg 4 is the net of cylinder C

76

171

Table I10 E2 Mathematics Test. Percentage of children answering each item correctly

Item number	Percentage of correct answers	Item number	Percentage of correct answers
1 (Aa)	94	26 (K)	40
2 (Ab)	84	27 (F)	64
3	87	28	60
4	96	29	76
5	92	30	49
6	82	31	18
7	86	32	62
8 (C)	92	33	55
9	78	34	60
10	72	35	54
11	80	36	52
12	86	37	42
13	15	38	23
14 (B)	83	39	42
15 (D)	59	40	34
16	57	41	37
17 (E)	47	42 (G)	37
18	41	43	17
19 (J)	69	44	30
20 (N)	76	45 (M)	28
21 (L)	49	46	35
22	45	47	20
23	71	48	27
24	31	49	19
25 (I)	61	50 (H)	20

Note: The letters shown after fourteen of the item numbers correspond to the test items reproduced in Appendix I

APPENDIX J. THE TEACHING OF FRENCH

103 As was explained in the preface, the teaching of French was not given high priority in the survey because a substantial report[1] has recently been published on the subject.

104 The sample of schools in this survey does not include any where French was taught to 7 year old children.

105 At 9 years of age 7 per cent of the schools taught French. Of these schools two-thirds were separate junior schools. Only one class was in an inner city area, three were in rural areas and the remainder, 27, were in 'other urban' areas.

[1] Dr Clare Burstall. *Primary French in the balance.* NFER, 1974

106 French was taught in 25 per cent of 11 year old classes overall. In 'other urban' areas French was taught to 36 per cent of the 11 year old classes and in inner city areas to 9 per cent.

107 For the teaching of French to be effective in primary schools it has been suggested that it should be taught daily for at least 20 to 30 minutes, thereby totalling between $1\frac{1}{2}$ and $2\frac{1}{2}$ hours each week. This was done in about a quarter of the classes that taught French; the remaining classes gave less than $1\frac{2}{3}$ hours a week to the subject.

Annex A Survey documents

1 Letter sent to heads prior to the survey inspection.
2 Table requiring completion sent to heads prior to the preliminary visit.
3 Head's questionnaire.
4 Staffing questionnaire: to be completed by head.
5 Class teacher's questionnaire.
6 Notes to questionnaires.

LETTER SENT TO HEADS PRIOR TO THE SURVEY INSPECTION

Department of Education and Science
Elizabeth House York Road London SE1 7PH

Telegrams Aristides London   Telex 23171

Telephone 01-928 9222 ext 2111

Your reference	
Our reference	INS 49/12/010/06
Date	December 1975

Dear

NATIONAL SURVEY OF PRIMARY EDUCATION

During the Autumn Term 1974 and the Spring Term 1975 HM Inspectorate carried out a study to test the feasibility of evaluating the education of a representative sample of children at certain stages in the primary school. The main purpose was to test survey procedures in terms of both the load they imposed on the schools visited and their effectiveness for assessment purposes. The schools in the feasibility were, of course, too few to allow any generalisations to be drawn from the findings. It now seems clear that the procedures worked well enough to allow a general survey to go ahead. Local authority and teachers' associations have been kept informed about both the feasibility and the main exercises. The latter began towards the end of October 1975.

Your school has been selected for the main survey as one of a statistical, national sample of 542 primary schools in England. As we explained to the LEAs and schools involved in the feasibility study, HMIs will be carrying out certain inspection procedures but there will be no reporting on individual schools or groups of schools in an LEA.

Within each school the survey will concentrate, where the age range allows, on three classes: one containing 7 year old children, one containing 9 year-olds, and one containing 11 year-olds. The classes will be selected at random. Information will be collected in three main ways. Before the visit of the team you and the teachers of the classes concerned will be asked to complete questionnaires. At the time of the visit the selected classes will be inspected by two HMIs. The third source of information will be the results of objective tests administered by the National Foundation for Educational Research.

The precise arrangements for these tests are still under consideration. They will not, ordinarily, be given at the time of the inspection. They will probably be distributed to schools during May of the school year in which the inspection takes place. They will consist of tests of reading for 9 and 11 year-olds and of mathematics for 11 year-olds. It is expected that only a sample of children in each group will be tested.

1.

The inspection will be concerned with the balance of activities undertaken by pupils and their suitability as judged by the competence of the children to do what is being asked of them. The HMI team will be particularly interested in the following broad areas of the curriculum: Language and literacy, mathematics, science, aesthetics (including physical and practical aspects of education), social development (including historical and geographical ideas).

The visits have been arranged to leave time for discussion about the organisation of the school and the work observed with yourself and with such other members of staff as seems appropriate.

This visit will not take the form of a traditional full inspection of your school, but the fact that we are looking in depth at certain age groups will give us a detailed view of their work and the organisation behind it. This will contribute towards the build-up of a national picture of the education of 7, 9 and 11 year old children in primary schools in England.

We expect the survey visit to be on ....

I plan to call in to see you on ...., if that is a suitable date. We can then discuss the arrangements for the survey, the procedure for the random selection of the classes, and answer any queries you or your staff may have. I should be glad if you would kindly complete the attached table before I come so that we can then decide upon the classes to be seen.

Yours sincerley

Enc

TABLE REQUIRING COMPLETION SENT TO HEADS PRIOR TO THE PRELIMINARY VISIT

PRIMARY SURVEY: TABLE 1

Please complete the following table by entering the number of children in the appropriate space.

NOTE: i. Exclude a. All children attending PART-TIME.

              b. Pupils attending special units attached to the school eg unit for maladjusted children.

    ii. Include: all other children who are AT PRESENT on the school roll and attending FULL TIME.

    iii. Children should be categorised according to their age at the END of the current school year (31 August, next).

    iv. If any class has a special function ie remedial class, class for particularly gifted children; please place an asterisk (°) against the class number.

The following two notes will apply only in unusual cases

         v. FULL TIME pupils in the 4+ age group to be included in the 5+ group.

         vi. FULL TIME pupils who will be 13 or more at the end of the current school year to be included in the 12+ group.

Class Number	Age at end of School Year								Class Total
	Infant			Junior				Secondary	
	5+	6+	7+	8+	9+	10+	11+	12+	
1									
2									
3									
4									
5									
6									
7									
8									
9									
10									
11									
12									
13									
14									
15									
16									
17									
18									
19									
20									
21									
22									
23									
24									
25									
26									
27									
28									
29									
30									

HEAD'S QUESTIONNAIRE

NATIONAL PRIMARY SURVEY

Form 2

Sheet 1 of 10

Form Number

1	2
Ø	2

School Code (for survey)

3	4	5	6
P			

HEAD TEACHERS QUESTIONNAIRE

Please complete the details of your school requested below. This information is for clerical checking purposes only and it will NOT be computerised.

1. Name of Head ....

2. Name of School ....

3. Address of School ....

   ....

   ....

4. Telephone Number ....

Please supply the following for computer use:

5. Local Education Authority Number ....

7	8	9

6. School Number ....

10	11	12	13

NATIONAL PRIMARY SURVEY

COMPLETION INSTRUCTIONS

i.   Answers are indicated by placing figures in the numbered boxes provided in the right hand margin.

ii. Do not enter more than one figure in any numbered box.

iii. Every box of the form ⌷ should be completed.   YOU ARE ASKED NEVER TO LEAVE ONE OF THESE BOXES BLANK.

iv. Boxes of the form ☐ are optional boxes.   The question rubric will make it clear that you may leave such boxes blank in certain cases.

v.   Please do not leave an optional box blank unless the question rubric specifically allows this.

vi. To avoid ambiguity please observe the following conventions:

Write zero as 0̸ to avoid confusion with 6.

Write seven as 7̸ to avoid confusion with 2.

Write one as I to avoid confusion with 2.

vii. If you should make an incorrect entry in a box, cross out the incorrect entry, and substitute the correct one.   If this is not possible, cross out the entire box and draw a new box with the correct sequence number and the correct entry in it.   Do not attempt to alter incorrect entries.

viii. It is not anticipated that you will find difficulty in answering the questions, but if a case of particular difficulty does occur, please make a pencilled comment to this effect and discuss the matter with HMIs when they make the visit.

P ☐ ⌢ ☐

179

NATIONAL PRIMARY SURVEY

For Questions 7, 8 and 9 please enter 001, 002, ... 010, 011, ... 100, 101 etc as appropriate, eg enter 79 as 079.

The questions refer to children at present on the school roll except for those in special units attached to the school eg unit for maladjusted children, unit for partially hearing children. Children in such units should be excluded.

7. *Number of children attending full time.*

8. *Number of children attending part time. If none enter 000.*

9. *Total number on roll (Answer 7 + Answer 8). Please complete this, even if the answer is the same as for Question 7.*

10. *Please indicate which age groups are taught in your school, as follows:*

If the age group is taught in your school		*enter 1*
If the age group is not taught in your school		*enter 2*

Age at END of Current School Year	*Status*
5+	*Infants*
6+	*Infants*
7+	*Top Year Infants*
8+	*1st Year Junior*
9+	*2nd Year Junior*
10+	*3rd Year Junior*
11+	*Top Year Junior*
12+	*1st Year Secondary*

14
17
20

23
24
25
26
27
28
29
30

P

180

NATIONAL PRIMARY SURVEY

11. For each of the following age groups, if it is taught in your school, give the number in the age group at present. (Ages as at 31 August next).

Please enter 001, 002, ..., 010, 011, ... 100, 101, etc as appropriate, eg enter 79 as 079.

	Age Group
	7+
	9+
	11+

31
34
37

12. a. Is the school "one form entry" or less at the age group 7+?

If none in 7+ age group)
)
or) enter 1 and go to Question 13
)
If one form entry or less)

In other cases   enter 2 and go to 12.b.

40

b. If the 7+ age group is streamed BY ABILITY enter 1; if unstreamed enter 2.

41

13. a. Is the school "one form entry" or less at the age group 9+?

If none in 9+ age group)
)
or) enter 1 and go to Question 14
)
If one form entry or less)

In other cases   enter 2 and go to 13.b.

42

b. If the 9+ age group is streamed BY ABILITY enter 1; if unstreamed enter 2.

43

14. a. Is the school "one form entry" or less at the age group 11+?

If none in 11+ age group)
)
or) enter 1 and go to Question 15
)
If one form entry or less)

In other cases   enter 2 and go to 14.b.

44

b. If the 11+ age group is streamed BY ABILITY enter 1; if unstreamed enter 2.

45

15. Are any teachers involved in co-operative teaching? ie Are two or more teachers collaborating to teach one year group, or other organisational unit, in one teaching space?

If yes   enter 1

If no   enter 2

46

P

181

NATIONAL PRIMARY SURVEY

16. Has your school been open for at least six COMPLETED terms?

    If yes   enter 6

    If no   enter the number of completed terms as 0, 1, 2, ... , 5

47 ☐

For Questions 17, 18, 19: Omit teachers who are solely concerned with teaching children in special units. The questions refer to the last six completed terms; if your school has not been open that long you should answer for the number of completed terms it has been open.

If none, please enter 00. Otherwise enter 01, 02, ... 10, 11 etc as appropriate.

17. How many of the teachers who joined the staff as full time members during the last six completed terms subsequently left during the same period?

48 ☐☐

18. How many teachers have left during the last six completed terms? (Including those in Question 17 above).

50 ☐☐

19. How many probationers are there on the staff at present?

52 ☐☐

20. Please enter the approximate PERCENTAGE of children on roll whose first language is one of the following. In each case, if none enter 00. Otherwise enter 01, 02, ... 10, 11 etc as appropriate. [Rounding up to the nearest whole number.]

Punjabi . . . . 54 ☐☐

Gujerati . . . . 56 ☐☐

Bengali . . . . 58 ☐☐

Other Indian or Pakistani Languages . . . . 60 ☐☐

Italian . . . . 62 ☐☐

Turkish . . . . 64 ☐☐

Greek . . . . 66 ☐☐

Spanish . . . . 68 ☐☐

Other European Languages (EXCLUDING English) . . . . 70 ☐☐

Any African Language . . . . 72 ☐☐

Chinese . . . . 74 ☐☐

Other . . . . 76 ☐☐

NOTE: West Indians are catered for by Question 21 overleaf.

P ☐☐☐

NATIONAL PRIMARY SURVEY

21. Please enter the approximate PERCENTAGE of children on roll whose speech patterns are a result of West Indian connections in the family.

   If none, please enter *00*.   Otherwise enter *01, 02, ... 10, 11 etc as appropriate.   [Rounding up to the nearest whole number.]

   78 [|]

22. Are any of the following records used to facilitate the transfer of children between your school and the next?

   If yes   *enter 1*

   If no   *enter 2*

   The school's own type of record for individual pupils   80 [ ]

   Folders of work samples of individual pupils   81 [ ]

   Official Local Education Authority record cards   82 [ ]

23. Are any of the following procedures used to facilitate the transfer of pupils between your school and the next?

   If yes   *enter 1*

   If no   *enter 2*

   Pupils visiting before transfer ....   83 [ ]

   Staff occasionally visiting ....   84 [ ]

   Staff regularly visiting ....   85 [ ]

   Staff exchange for teaching commitment ....   86 [ ]

   Joint meetings of staff for curriculum discussions ....   87 [ ]

   Head teachers visiting ....   88 [ ]

   Feedback of comment on your children's subsequent progress ......   89 [ ]

P [| |]

NATIONAL PRIMARY SURVEY

24. *Are there written guide lines, or written schemes of work for the following aspects of curriculum?*

      If yes   *enter 1*

      If no   *enter 2*

Language development..	90
Art	91
Crafts	92
R.E.	93
History	94
Geography	95
Science	96
Mathematics	97
Music	98
Gymnastics	99
Dance	100
Games	101
Swimming	102
Drama	103
French	104
Social Studies...	105
Environmental studies	106
Humanities	107
Health Education	108
Others	109

P

184

Narrative replies

25. Please suggest three aspects in order of importance which, in your view, should be given greater emphasis in future patterns of initial teacher training.

26. Please give details of up to three courses that you have attended and found useful.

    Please code the boxes to indicate the type of course.

If one lecture	1
If several lectures on separate days	2
If a single whole day course	3
If more than one full day but less than 11	4
If more than 10 full days but less than one term	5
If one term or more	6

TITLE OF COURSE	ORGANISED BY	CODE
. . . .	. . . .	
. . . .	. . . .	
. . . .	. . . .	

27. Please add any suggestions you may wish to offer concerning the need for future in-service courses.

P

NATIONAL PRIMARY SURVEY

Form 2

Sheet 9 of 10

Narrative Replies

28. Please state, as briefly as possible, what the school sets out to achieve in the following aspects of the curriculum.

Language and Literacy

Mathematics

Science

Social and Moral Education

Aesthetic awareness and experience

P			

186

NATIONAL PRIMARY SURVEY

Form 2

Sheet 10 of 10

Narrative Replies

29. ¯ *Please list briefly any ways in which parents are involved in the life of the school.*

30. *Please add any comments or suggestions you may wish to make with particular reference to aspects of the organisation of your school which you consider have been overlooked in this questionnaire.*

P			

STAFFING QUESTIONNAIRE: TO BE COMPLETED BY HEAD

NATIONAL PRIMARY SURVEY

Form 3

Sheet 1 of 5

Form Number

1	2
Ø	3

STAFFING

(To be completed by the Head Teacher)

SCHOOL CODE (for survey)

3	4	5	6
P			

(1)

NATIONAL PRIMARY SURVEY

Please complete one line of the table for yourself (line 01) and one line for each member of your staff (full time and part time). Do not include members of staff in special units.

DATA REQUIREMENTS

Column A — Using the following codes, please indicate which teachers are involved in the survey.

CODE

for the teachers not involved	0
for the teacher of the 7+ class visited	1
for the teacher of the 9+ class visited	2
for the teacher of the 11+ class visited	3
for the Head Teacher (pre-printed as teacher No.1)	4

Column B — Use the following codes to indicate sex

Male	1
Female	2

Column C — Using the following codes, please indicate the scale of the present post.

CODE

for Head Teacher (pre-printed as teacher No.1)	99
for Deputy Head	88
for Scale 1 post	01
for Scale 2 post	02

etc.

Column D — Use the following codes to indicate qualifications.

CODE

for B/Ed	1
for Graduate other than B/Ed	2
for all other cases	3

Column E — Enter the number of completed TERMS of teaching as 01, 02, ... 10, 11 etc as appropriate.

NOTE: If the answer is 90 or more — enter 90.

Column F — Enter the number of completed TERMS at present school as 01, 02, ... 10, 11 etc as appropriate.

NOTE: If the answer is 90 or more — enter 90.

189

NATIONAL PRIMARY SURVEY

Form 3
Sheet 3 of 5

Column G

Please enter code 10 (ie 10 half days) for each teacher in FULL-TIME service.

For teachers serving PART-TIME enter the full time equivalent, to the nearest half day.

eg A teacher attending each morning session: code 05.
A teacher attending one full day and one half day per week: code 03.

Column H

If the teacher has no special curricular responsibility please put zero (0) in all six boxes. Otherwise enter up to three of the following codes to indicate responsibilities. Any unused pairs of boxes should be filled with zeros (0).

[If more than three curricular responsibilities enter the three most important ones.]

Responsible for:	CODE
Language development	01
Art	02
Crafts	03
R.E.	04
History	05
Geography	06
Science	07
Mathematics	08
Music	09
Gymnastics	10
Dance	11
Games	12
Swimming	13
Drama	14
French	15
Social studies	16
Environmental studies	17
Humanities	18
Health Education	19
Other	20

NATIONAL PRIMARY SURVEY

Form 3
Sheet 4 of 5

Column I

If the teacher has no special organisational responsibility please put zero (0) in all six boxes. Otherwise enter up to three of the following codes to indicate responsibilities. Any unused pairs of boxes should be filled with zeros (0).

[If more than three organisational responsibilities enter the three most important ones.]

Responsible for:	CODE
Nursery unit	51
Infant department	52
Junior department	53
Library	54
Resource centre	55
Home/School liaison	56
Liaison with other schools	57
Year group leader or co-ordinator	58
Team leader or co-ordinator	59
Remedial work	60
Needs of the very able	61
Other	62

NATIONAL PRIMARY SURVEY

PUNCH-ROOM.   *Punch one record per line, duplicating the six characters quoted for reference below.*

		A	B		C	D	E		F		G		H						I					
Staff		Involvement	Sex	Scale of present post		Qualifications	Number of completed terms of teaching		Time at present school in completed terms		Full or Part Time		Special Curricular Responsibility						Special Organisational Responsibility					
													1		2		3		1		2		3	
7	8	9	10	11	12	13	14	15	16	17	18	19	20	21	22	23	24	25	26	27	28	29	30	31
0	1	4		9	9																			
0	2																							
0	3																							
0	4																							
0	5																							
0	6																							
0	7																							
0	8																							
0	9																							
1	0																							
1	1																							
1	2																							
1	3																							
1	4																							
1	5																							
1	6																							
1	7																							
1	8																							
1	9																							
2	0																							
2	1																							
2	2																							
2	3																							
2	4																							
2	5																							
2	6																							
2	7																							
2	8																							
2	9																							
3	0																							

	1	2
	0	3

Form Number

School Code (for survey)

3	4	5	6
P			

CLASS TEACHER'S QUESTIONNAIRE

NATIONAL PRIMARY SURVEY

Form 4

Sheet 1 of 13

1	**2**
Ø	4

Form Number

3	**4**	**5**	**6**
P			·

School Code (for survey)

7	**8**
Ø	9

Age Group Code

CLASS TEACHER'S QUESTIONNAIRE

An Introduction to the Survey:

Your class has been selected as one of about 1200 classes drawn from a sample of over 500 schools throughout England for the National Primary Survey.

This questionnaire requests certain information about your class and its organisation. Your answers will contribute towards the build-up of a national picture of the education of 7, 9 and 11 year old children in primary schools in England and it is vital for the success of the survey that every one of the many people involved responds fully and accurately.

Your name is not recorded on this or any other survey document. Once all the data has been assembled for central processing it will be impossible to identify you directly.

NATIONAL PRIMARY SURVEY

COMPLETION INSTRUCTIONS

i. Answers are indicated by placing figures in the numbered boxes provided in the right hand margin.

ii. Do not enter more than one figure in any numbered box.

iii. Every box of the form ⊔ should be completed. YOU ARE ASKED NEVER TO LEAVE ONE OF THESE BOXES BLANK.

iv. Boxes of the form ⊔ are optional boxes. The question rubric will make it clear that you may leave such boxes blank in certain cases.

v. Please do not leave an optional box blank unless the question rubric specifically allows this.

vi. To avoid ambiguity please observe the following conventions:

Write zero as Ø to avoid confusion with 6.

Write seven as 7̸ to avoid confusion with 2.

Write one as I to avoid confusion with 2.

vii. If you should make an incorrect entry in a box, cross out the incorrect entry and substitute the correct one. If this is not possible, cross out the entire box and draw a new box with the correct sequence number and the correct entry in it. Do not attempt to alter incorrect entries.

viii. It is not anticipated that you will find difficulty in answering the questions but if a case of particular difficulty does occur please make a pencilled comment to this effect and discuss the matter with HMIs when they make the visit.

1. Does your class contain children of more than one academic year group?

     If yes   enter 1 and go to Questions 2 and 3

     If no   enter 2 and go to Question 4

9 ☐

2. Is the fact that you have children of more than one academic year group in your class a direct result of the small total number on the school roll?

     If yes   enter 1

     If no   enter 2

10 ☐

3. Please indicate the age range of your class by entering the code for the statement which most nearly represents the current situation.

     The majority of the children are of one academic year group but there are a few children of a different year group (or groups)   enter 1

     OR

     The children are from two academic year groups, with significant numbers in each of the two years (and possibly a few children from another group or groups)   enter 2

     OR

     The children are from three or more academic year groups with significant numbers in at least three groups   enter 3

11 ☐

4. Is your class involved in "setting" or regrouping arrangments with other classes?

     If yes   enter 1 and go to Question 5

     If no   enter 2 and go to Question 6

12 ☐

P ☐☐☐

NATIONAL PRIMARY SURVEY

5. Are the following aspects of curriculum involved in setting or re-grouping arrangements with other classes?

<table>
<tr><td>If yes</td><td>enter 1</td><td></td></tr>
<tr><td>If no</td><td>enter 2</td><td></td></tr>
<tr><td>Language development; listening ....</td><td>13</td><td></td></tr>
<tr><td>talking.....................................</td><td>14</td><td></td></tr>
<tr><td>reading.....................................</td><td>15</td><td></td></tr>
<tr><td>writing.....................................</td><td>16</td><td></td></tr>
<tr><td>Mathematics ....</td><td>17</td><td></td></tr>
<tr><td>Music ....</td><td>18</td><td></td></tr>
<tr><td>Art ....</td><td>19</td><td></td></tr>
<tr><td>Craft.....................................</td><td>20</td><td></td></tr>
<tr><td>P.E. ....</td><td>21</td><td></td></tr>
<tr><td>Humanities ....</td><td>22</td><td></td></tr>
<tr><td>Science ....</td><td>23</td><td></td></tr>
<tr><td>Other Aspects ....</td><td>24</td><td></td></tr>
</table>

6. Is your class taught by other members of staff (not peripatetic teachers) whilst you are working elsewhere in the school? ie whilst you are teaching another class or having a non-teaching period.

    If yes   enter 1 and go to Questions 7 and 8

    If no   enter 2 and go to Question 9   25

7. Please give the number of other members of staff who take your class. Enter 01, 02, ... 10, 11 etc as appropriate.   26

P

195

NATIONAL PRIMARY SURVEY

8. *Please complete a line for each member of staff who takes your class whilst you are elsewhere in the school.*

Start at line 01 and leave any unused lines blank.

NOTE: You may use a subject code more than once. If a member of staff takes your class for more than one subject complete one line for each subject taken by him/her.

Please use the following codes to indicate subject taught:

	CODE
Language development	*01*
Art	*02*
Crafts	*03*
R.E.	*04*
History	*05*
Geography	*06*
Science	*07*
Mathematics	*08*
Music	*09*
Gymnastics	*10*
Dance	*11*
Games	*12*
Swimming	*13*
Drama	*14*
French	*15*
Social studies	*16*
Environmental studies	*17*
Humanities	*18*
Health education	*19*
Others	*20*

Please enter 01, 02, ... 10, 11 etc as appropriate for the number of times per week.

Please enter the total time per week in hours, as follows:

	ENTER
Up to and including 1 hour	*01*
More than 1, up to and including 2 hours	*02*
More than 2, up to and including 3 hours	*03*
More than 3, up to and including 4 hours	*04*
More than 4, up to and including 5 hours	*05*
More than 5, up to and including 6 hours	*06*
More than 6, up to and including 7 hours	*07*
More than 7, up to and including 8 hours	*08*
More than 8, up to and including 9 hours	*09*
More than 9, up to and including 10 hours	*10*
More than 10, up to and including 15 hours	*15*
More than 15 hours	*20*

eg 3 hours 40 minutes entered as 04
1 hour 5 minutes entered as 02

Please do NOT round to the nearest hour eg 2 hours 15 minutes is coded as 3, not 2.

Line Number	Subject Taught	Number of times class taken per week	Total time per week spent with class
28 0 1			
36 0 2			
44 0 3			
52 0 4			
60 0 5			
68 0 6			
76 0 7			
84 0 8			
92 0 9			
100 1 0			

P

NATIONAL PRIMARY SURVEY

9. Do you group the children within your class in any way?

     If yes   *enter 1 and go to Questions 10 and 11*

     If no   *enter 2 and go to Question 12*

108 ☐

10. Please indicate the method of grouping by entering the code for the statement which most nearly represents the current organisation of the class.

                                               ENTER

     As a regular feature of class organisation groups are selected according to subject eg a pupil may be in one group for reading but in a different one for mathematics.   1

   OR

     Work is not normally organised for groups but they are sometimes formed or re-formed according to the needs of the moment.   2

   OR

     Once the class has been divided into groups all group work is carried out in these groups no matter which area of the curriculum is being studied.   3

109 ☐

11. Please indicate the dominant characteristic by which groups are formed for the aspects of the curriculum listed below.

     CHARACTERISTIC

If by ability	enter 1
If by mixed ability	enter 2
If by friendship	enter 3
If by shared interests	enter 4
If by sex	enter 5
If by age	enter 6
If NOT GROUPED	enter 7

Language development; listening	110 ☐
talking	111 ☐
reading	112 ☐
writing	113 ☐
Mathematics	114 ☐
Music	115 ☐
Art	116 ☐
Crafts	117 ☐
P.E.	118 ☐
Humanities	119 ☐
Science	120 ☐
Other Aspects	121 ☐

P ☐ ☐ ☐

197

NATIONAL PRIMARY SURVEY

12. Does some of the work by pupils take the form of individual assignments?

      If yes   *enter 1 and proceed to Question 13*

      If no   *enter 2 and proceed to Question 14*

122 ☐

13. Do the individual assignments apply to the following aspects of curriculum?

      If frequently   *enter 1*
      If infrequently   *enter 2*
      If never   *enter 3*

Language development; listening 123

              talking 124

              reading 125

              writing 126

Mathematics 127

Music 128

Art 129

Crafts 130

P.E. 131

Humanities 132

Science 133

Other aspects 134

14. Please indicate whether the following aspects of school organisation currently affect your class, with particular reference to the teaching of pupils in need of extra help, including remedial teaching. [Do not include exceptionally able children, who are catered for by Question 15.]

      If yes   *enter 1*

      If no   *enter 2*

Withdrawal of individuals 135

Withdrawal of groups 136

Long term withdrawal to a special class 137

Supernumerary teacher, working within the class, in addition to yourself. ... 138

Co-operative ways of working between yourself and other teachers to allow regrouping of two or more classes 139

P ☐☐☐

198

NATIONAL PRIMARY SURVEY

Form 4

Sheet 8 of 13

PUNCH-ROOM

15. Please indicate whether the following aspects of school organisation currently affect your class, with particular reference to the teaching of exceptionally able children.

If yes enter 1
If no enter 2

Withdrawal of individuals	140
Withdrawal of groups	141
Long term withdrawal to a special class	142
Supernumerary teacher, working within the class, in addition to yourself	143
Co-operative ways of working between yourself and other teachers to allow regrouping of two or more classes	144

16. Are any children in your class taught by peripatetic teachers?

If yes give the number of teachers by entering *01, 02,* . . . . . *10,* 11 etc as appropriate and go to Question 17

If no enter *00* and go to Question 18   145

17. Are peripatetic teachers employed with your class for the following purposes?

If with the whole class enter 1
If with part of the class enter 2
If not enter 3

French	147
Instrumental teaching; strings	148
woodwind	149
brass	150
piano	151
others	152
General musical activities	153
Mathematics	154
Reading	155
Writing	156
Other language skills	157
English as a second language	158
Art	159
Needlework	160
Cookery	161
P.E.	162
Other crafts	163
Other subjects	164

P

NATIONAL PRIMARY SURVEY

18. Do you have PAID adult help in your classroom?

    If yes   enter 1 and go to Question 19

    If no   enter 2 and go to Question 20

    165 ☐

19. Please complete a line for each paid helper. If there are more than 4 enter the 4 who spend most time with your class.

    Number of hours per week: Use the grouping shown for Question 8.

    Nature of Duties: (Columns A, B and C).

    If yes   enter 1

    If no   enter 2

    Column A: Directly involved with the children's learning
    Column B: Involved with children's welfare
    Column C: Involved with preparing materials and resources

Helper	Hours per week	A	B	C
166				
172				
178				
184				

20. Do you have VOLUNTARY help from parents in your classroom?

    If yes   enter 1 and go to Questions 21 and 22

    If no   enter 2 and go to Question 23

    190 ☐

21. Please give the average number of parents per week helping in your classroom. Enter 01, 02, ... 10, 11 etc as appropriate.

    191 ☐☐

22. Please indicate the nature of the parents' involvement.

    If yes   enter 1

    If no   enter 2

    Directly involved with your children's learning during school hours ....   **193** ☐

    Involved with your children's welfare in the school (including supervisory help on school visits) ....   **194** ☐

    Involved with preparing materials and resources for your children ....   **195** ☐

    Other kinds of involvement with your children ....   **196** ☐

P ☐☐☐

200

NATIONAL PRIMARY SURVEY

23. Did you use the following to assess the capabilities of your class, when the children first came to you?

    If yes   *enter 1*

    If no   *enter 2*

School's (or previous school's) individual records   197

Individual folders of work samples   198

Class lists   199

Visiting the class when they were with the previous teacher   200

Discussion with previous teachers   201

Objective tests   202

Tests devised within the school   203

24. Do you use standardised tests which give attainment scores, ages or quotients?

    If yes   enter 1 and go to Question 25

    If no   enter 2 and go to Question 26   204

25. Do you use standardised tests for diagnostic purposes ie to reveal details of learning difficulties?

    If yes   *enter 1*

    If no   *enter 2*   205

26. Please indicate, as follows, the phase for which you were initially trained.

                                          CODE

Nursery or Infants 1

Infants only 2

First school 3

Infants/Junior 4

Junior only 5

Junior/Secondary 6

Middle school 7

Secondary only 8

Other training 9   206

P

NATIONAL PRIMARY SURVEY

27. *Is your classroom on a separate site from the main school building?*

    If yes   *enter 1*

    If no   *enter 2*

28. *Is your classroom in hutted accommodation?*

    If yes   *enter 1*

    If no   *enter 2*

29. *Please enter the code for the statement which most accurately describes the teaching space in which you work.*

    A separate classroom   *enter 1*

    A space shared by two classes   *enter 2*

    A space shared by three or more classes   *enter 3*

, 9+,

NATIONAL PRIMARY SURVEY

Form 4

Sheet 12 of 13

Narrative Replies

30. *Please suggest up to three aspects which should, in your view, be given greater emphasis in future patterns of initial training.*

31. *Please list up to three in-service courses attended which you have found most useful in your present work.*

   Please code the boxes to indicate the type of course.

	CODE
If one lecture	*1*
If several lectures on separate days	*2*
If a single whole day course	*3*
If more than one full day but less than 11	*4*
If more than ten full days but less than one term	*5*
If one term or more	*6*

TITLE OF COURSE	ORGANISED BY	CODE
. . . .	. . . .	
. . . .	. . . .	
. . . .	. . . .	

9+,

NATIONAL PRIMARY SURVEY

Form
Sheet 4

Sheet 13 of 13

Narrative Replies

32. *Please add any suggestions which you may wish to offer concerning the need for future in-service courses.*

33. *Please add any comments or suggestions you may wish to make, with particular reference to aspects of the organisation of your class which you consider have not been covered in this questionnaire.*

Notes to questionnaires

1 The code number was entered on questionnaires before they were issued.

2 The staffing questionnaire: additional information was sought to cover situations where the head taught one of the survey classes, and where a teacher taught two of the survey groups. In practice only the former situation occurred with any frequency.

The following codes, additional to those in the staff questionnaire under 'Data requirements – column A', were supplied to heads with appropriate instructions.

Code	Situation
5	Head takes 11 year old teaching group.
6	Head takes 11 and 9 year old teaching groups.
7	Head takes 9 and 7 year old teaching groups.
8	Classteacher takes 11 and 9 year old teaching groups.
9	Classteacher takes 9 and 7 year old teaching groups.
A	Head takes 9 year old teaching group.
B	Head takes 7 year old teaching group.
C	Classteacher takes 11 and 7 year old teaching groups.
D	Head takes 11 and 7 year old teaching groups.
E	Head takes all three teaching groups.

3 The classteacher's questionnaire shown relates to 9 year old classes. Apart from the age group code the questionnaire was identical for 7 year and 11 year old classes.

4 The original question 16 in the classteacher's questionnaire read, 'Do you have peripatetic teachers working in your class?'. This was found to be ambiguous since some classteachers, quite reasonably, took this to mean that they should only include peripatetic teachers actually present in their classroom. This was not intended. The revised question, as shown in the questionnaire in the annex, was used from the third term onwards; the data from this question for the first two terms were discarded. The figures were weighted to take account of this.

Annex B   HMI schedules

1 For the purpose of this survey HM Inspectors made their assessments in accordance with agreed schedules. These schedules listed a wide range of activities likely to be found in primary schools, so that a record of what was done in a variety of individual classes could be made and in order that the material could subsequently be dealt with statistically. The schedules were the same for all 7, 9 and 11 year old classes and regardless of the special circumstances of the school. It was not expected that any individual class would undertake activities relating to all the items listed in the schedules but that teachers make a selection from these according to the age and abilities of the pupils and the particular circumstances of the school. Six schedules were used and covered the following aspects of the work and organisation:

a. aesthetic education, including art and crafts, music and physical education

b. language and literacy

c. mathematics

d. experimental and observational science

e. social abilities, including history, geography and religious education

f. the organisation and methods of working including some aspects of the general provision in the school which influenced children's work.

Scales and 'match' assessments

2 To enable HMI's assessments and observations to be quantified, a number of scales were used. The following are examples of these scales.

i. The extent to which children made use of book collections or libraries as a starting point or resource to develop and extend language, whether spoken, written or through reading was recorded on a scale which referred to over-use; an appropriate level of use; under-use; no evidence of use; not used.

ii. The quality of book collections or libraries was assessed as good; generally good but some poor areas; generally poor but some good areas; poor; or no evidence.

iii. The emphasis given to practical activities involving addition, subtraction, multiplication and division was recorded on a scale which referred to over-emphasis; appropriate level of emphasis; under-emphasis; no evidence; not given attention.

iv. The extent to which opportunities were taken to develop singing as an aspect of musical experience was recorded as taking place to a significant degree; to an insignificant degree; no evidence; or not given attention.

3 In assessing emphasis or significance HMI based their judgement on what experience has shown to be reasonable for children of a given age and ability. For example, in assessing whether opportunities were taken to develop gymnastics, dance, games or swimming to a significant degree, HMI took into account not only the age of the children and the time devoted to these activities but also other indicators such as the available resources, the pace of the work and the pupils' involvement and application.

4 The degree of 'match' between the standard of work the children were doing and that which they were considered by HMI to be capable of doing, as judged by their performance at the time of the inspection, was recorded in the following categories:

Considerable over-expectation
slight over-expectation ⎤ reasonably
good match   ⎬ satisfactory
slight under-expectation ⎦ match
considerable under-expectation.

5 HM Inspectors made their assessment on the basis of the observation of the work in progress, the inspection of previously completed work including the work in children's exercise books, discussions with teachers

and talking with children. The assessments were made separately for the most able, average and less able groups of children within each class as identified by their teachers.

6 Over-expectation was evident where children made too many mistakes and appeared to lack confidence; the level of the work was too difficult for the children and was remote from their previous experience and existing skills and knowledge; tasks set were beyond the understanding of the children and called for the mastery of skills and techniques which required a degree of sophistication that the children had not acquired. Over-expectation often led to children becoming discouraged and tentative in their approach to their work.

7 Under-expectation was recorded where there was evidence that the work required of children was too easily achieved and did not make appropriate demands on the children's developing capacity to observe, discriminate or make informed choices. Where there was insufficient stimulus in the tasks presented to the children the pace of work was sometimes slow because of boredom and easy distraction, or rushed because it required little thought; there was often a lackadaisical approach to the work, poor presentation and slipshod errors. In some cases the range of work was narrow and undemanding and children were not being introduced to skills and techniques which would normally be mastered by children at that age and level of ability. Under-expectation often took the form of children being required or allowed to repeat work already understood or mastered instead of being challenged by new skills and ideas.

8 A reasonably satisfactory match was recorded when there was evidence of ordered and planned progression building on existing knowledge and skills and leading to the acquisition of further skill, information or understanding. The tasks presented to children required the use of an appropriate range and variety of books and materials and there was evidence of increasing skill in recording observations and in the ability to discriminate and to evaluate evidence. Where a reasonably satisfactory match was achieved children were normally confident in their work and not afraid to make occasional errors which they regarded as a stimulus to further effort; children displayed a sense of purpose in their work and appeared to enjoy the challenge of increasing, though realistic, demands made upon them. Many children gained satisfaction from the mastery of new skills and techniques and often displayed considerable persistence in achieving standards which satisfied themselves and their teachers.

SUMMARY OF SCHEDULES

9 The following summarizes all the factors referred to in the HMI Schedules for the inspection of the survey classes.

Aesthetic and physical education

i. Art and crafts

1 The extent to which children make use of the following starting points and resources in the development of aesthetic awareness: the immediate outdoor environment, arrangements and displays inside the school and the classroom, natural and man-made objects, a range of media for two and three dimensional work, visits to local art galleries, exhibitions or museums, visits by local craftsmen or artists.

2 The quality of the following resources: the arrangements and displays within the classroom including man-made objects, a range of media for drawing and print-making, materials and textiles, three dimensional constructional materials.

3 The emphasis given to art and crafts within the whole curriculum.

4 Evidence that children are learning to observe carefully in relation to form, texture, pattern and colour.

5 Evidence that children may turn readily to paint, clay or other media when they have something to express which is personal to them.

6 Evidence of the use of form, texture, pattern and colour in children's work.

7 Evidence that children are learning to select materials with discrimination.

8 Evidence that the children are learning to handle tools, apparatus and materials carefully and safely and with a sense of fitness for their purpose.

9 The use made of drawing and modelling techniques and skills to record observations or information in other areas of the curriculum.

ii. Music

10 The extent to which children make use of the following starting points and resources for musical experience: recorded music, television, radio, untuned and tuned percussion instruments, visits to concerts or to hear outside choirs, visits to the school by musicians.

11 The emphasis given to music within the whole curriculum.

12 The extent to which opportunities are taken to develop singing, listening, the learning of notation and creative music-making as aspects of musical experience.

13 The quality of the songs chosen.

14 The extent to which music is related to other areas of the curriculum.

15 The provision for children in the class to play musical instruments.

iii. Physical education

16 The extent to which children make use of the following starting points and resources for physical education: television, radio, gymnastic equipment of all kinds, games equipment and associated small apparatus.

17 The emphasis given to the full range of movement activities within the whole curriculum.

18 The extent to which opportunities are taken to develop gymnastics, dance, games and swimming within the range of physical activities.

19 Evidence that the children are developing skilful performance in gymnastics, skill in games or a games-like context, awareness and sensitivity in the use of expressive movement.

Language and literacy

1 The extent to which children make use of the following starting points and resources to develop and extend their language, whether spoken, written or through reading:

a. experiences out of school which have not been planned by the school

b. experiences in school including the display of materials and objects, the keeping of animals and plants, imaginative play, constructional activities

c. book collections or libraries

d. television, radio, ciné film, slides, pre-recorded material for listening, tape recordings by the children

e. reading schemes and courses, assignment cards, language course kits, text books

f. stories and poems read or told by the teacher

g. visiting speakers

h. the immediate outdoor environment, visits and school journeys.

2 The quality of the following: the arrangement of displays, book collections or libraries, pre-recorded material for listening, ciné film and slides, assignment cards, stories and poems read by the teacher.

3 The extent to which opportunities are taken to develop the language used in other areas of the curriculum.

4 Evidence that children are being taught to do the following: follow instructions, follow the plot of a story, listen to poetry, comprehend the main ideas and the details in information they are given, follow a discussion or the line of an argument and contribute appropriately.

5 The emphasis given to talking between the children and teachers, and the children and other adults.

6 The emphasis given to informal discussion among children during the working day and the provision of more formal, structured arrangements for discussion and exchange between children.

7 Evidence that children are encouraged to expand their spoken responses, that new vocabulary is introduced, that the use of more precise description is achieved, that children are helped to frame pertinent questions and that

children are taught to use alternative and more appropriate structures in their talking.

i Reading

8 Evidence, where appropriate, that children's own speech is used to provide early reading material.

9 Evidence that the children's own writing is used as part of their early reading material.

10 The emphasis given to reading practice with main reading schemes and supplementary readers.

11 The emphasis given to the reading of fiction and non-fiction related to curricular work and other reading not related to curricular work.

12 The emphasis on the use of extended reading skills and children's comments on the material read.

13 The emphasis on the selection of books by the children themselves.

14 Evidence that children learn to turn readily and naturally to books for pleasure and that they use books with ease and confidence as a source of information.

15 Evidence that the children read poetry and that some of the children discuss books at more than a superficial level.

ii Writing

16 The emphasis given to self-chosen and prescribed topics for children's writing.

17 The emphasis given to self-chosen and prescribed topics related to other curricular areas.

18 The extent to which the following are used: copied writing, dictation and handwriting practice.

19 The extent to which descriptive, expressive, narrative and expository styles or modes of prose writing are used by the children.

20 The extent to which descriptive, expressive and narrative styles or modes of poetry writing are used by the children.

21 Evidence that the children's writing is used for the following purposes: to share information or experience with other children, as samples of work used by the teacher to monitor progress, as a basis for learning language, spelling, syntax and style.

22 Where French is taught, the number of sessions and total time per week which is spent on this subject.

Mathematics

1 The extent to which children make use of the following starting points and resources in the learning of mathematics:

    a. television and radio

    b. text books, commercial and school-made work cards

    c. investigations arising from questions asked by the children or initiated by the teachers

    d. practice of skills directed from the blackboard.

2 Evidence of sustained work on any mathematical topic.

3 Evidence of profitable links with other areas of the curriculum.

4 The emphasis given to the following aspects of mathematics during the current school year:

    a. qualitative mathematical description; unambiguous description of the properties of number, size, shape and position

    b. recognition of relationships and logical deduction applied to everyday things, geometrical shapes, number and ordering

c. appreciation of place value and recognition of simple number patterns (eg odds and evens, multiples, divisors, squares etc)

d. appreciation of some broader aspects of number (eg bases other than 10, number sequences, tests of divisibility)

e. use of various forms of visual presentation (eg three dimensional and diagrammatic forms, statistical charts, tables of data, networks etc)

f. use of models, maps, scale drawing etc

g. use of algebraic symbols; notations such as 'box' and arrow diagrams

h. sensible estimation and use of measurements of length, weight, area, volume and time

i. understanding of money and sense of values regarding simple purchases

j. quantitative description; sensible use of number in counting, describing and estimating

k. practical activities involving the ideas of $+$, $-$, $\times$ and $\div$

l. suitable calculations involving $+$, $-$, $\times$ and $\div$ with whole numbers

m. examples involving four rules of number including two places of decimals (as in pounds and pence and measures)

n. calculations involving the four rules applied to the decimal system

o. use of fractions (including the idea of equivalence) in the discussion of everyday things

p. competence in calculations involving the four rules applied to fractions.

Science

1 The extent to which children make use of the following starting points and resources in learning science:

a. children's experience out of school

b. experience of materials, plants and animals in school

c. television and radio

d. reference books, text books, commercial and school made assignment cards

e. the immediate outdoor environment.

2 Quality of the overall provision of resources for scientific investigation.

3 The emphasis given to science within the whole curriculum.

4 The quality of assignment cards, reference books and materials available for scientific investigation.

5 Evidence of investigations arising from questions asked by the children.

6 Evidence that the children are using description arising from direct observation.

7 Evidence that the children are learning about the following :

a. notions of stability and change in relation to living things and materials

b. knowledge of some of the characteristics of living things including differences and similarities

c. reproduction, growth and development in succeeding generations

d. forms of energy sources and storage

e. factors which influence personal and community health, including safety

f. respect and care for living things.

8 The extent to which children are encouraged to identify significant patterns (eg the way plants react to light, the way materials react to heat, bird migration, the position of leaves on a plant stem etc).

Social abilities

i. Social, moral and religious education

1 The extent to which situations are planned to encourage the development of moral and ethical values in the following aspects:

    a. the use of initiative and making informed choices

    b. the exercise of responsibility and self-assessment in behaviour and work

    c. emotional development and sympathetic identification with others

    d. respect for other people

    e. respect for plants and animals

    f. respect for things

    g. contribution and participation as a member of a group

    h. the exercise of qualities of leadership.

2 The extent to which most children appear to be involved in the development of religious ideas and moral or ethical rules and values during the school assembly.

3 The extent to which children learn about man's attempt to frame religious and moral or ethical rules and values in the following aspects of their work:

    a. history and geography

    b. the Old and New Testament

    c. writings of other religions

    d. myths and legends

    e. other literature and drama.

ii. Geography and history

4 The extent to which children make use of the following starting points and resources to develop historical and geographical awareness:

   a. the memories of people known to the children

   b. artefacts, historical documents and the use of historical aspects of the local area

   c. historical programmes on television and radio

   d. history text books, work cards or assignment cards

   e. stories with an historical setting

   f. history reference books

   g. weather study

   h. use of geographical features of the local area

   i. geographical programmes on television and radio

   j. geography text books, work cards or assignment cards

   k. stories with an interesting geographical setting

   l. geography reference books.

5 The quality of the content of school-made assignment cards for history and geography.

6 The quality of history and geography reference books.

7 The emphasis given to developing children's awareness and appreciation of the past.

8 The extent to which children are becoming aware of historical change and the casual factors in relation to people's material circumstances, the way people behaved and the things people believed in the past.

9 The degree to which children are engaged in the following activities:

   a. understanding the nature of historical statements

   b. developing sympathy with the predicament of other people

c. developing an awareness of the need for evidence.

10 The emphasis given to geographical aspects of children's learning within the whole curriculum.

11 The degree to which the following geographical aspects were included in children's work during the current academic year both within and outside the locality :

    a. population and settlements

    b. agriculture and industry

    c. transport

    d. geographical land features

    e. natural resources.

12 The extent to which the children's work reveals an appreciation of man's dependence on natural phenomena and resources.

13 Evidence that children are becoming familiar with maps of the locality, atlases and globes.

Organisation and methods of working

1 The emphasis given to cognitive, social, emotional and physical development as judged by the quality of the children's work.

2 The degree to which posts carrying particular organisational or curricular responsibilities influence the work of the school as a whole.

3 The extent to which didactic and exploratory approaches to teaching were observed in the survey classes.

4 Evidence of effective inter-action between the basic skills of numeracy and literacy and the more imaginative aspects of the children's work.

5 Evidence that children are encouraged to follow a sustained interest in the course of their work.

6 The extent to which a quiet working atmosphere is established when this is appropriate.

7 The degree of control over the children's use of resources in the classroom.

8 The degree to which the content of the children's work is prescribed by the teacher.

9 Evidence that satisfactory educational use is made of spontaneous incidents which may arise.

10 The attention given to creating an intellectually stimulating environment inside and outside the school.

11 Evidence that vandalism outside school hours limits the creation of an aesthetically pleasing environment.

12 The extent to which the accommodation facilities or inhibits the children's work.

13 The extent to which the adequacy of resources facilitates or inhibits the children's work.

14 Type of catchment area and whether there is evidence of marked social difficulties.

Index

Major references are set in bold type

standards: 7.34, 8.51, 8.52
turnover: 7.4
standards of work: 5.84, 6.1, 6.20, 6.21,
8.39

statistical techniques: 1.8
stories, use of: 5.20, 5.22, 5.42, 5.119,
5.126, 7.8, 7.30
students: 8.35, 8.56, 8.57
study, extended: 3.22
survey, design: 1.1
swimming: 4.3, 5.106, 5.108, 6.5
syntax: 5 38, 5.45 8.20

T

teachers: **2.8–2.20**
 centres: 5.82
 class: 1.6, 1.8, 3.11, 3.14, 5.49, 6.11,
8.41
 deployment of: **3.11–3.14, 8.48, 8.52**
 difficulties experienced: 8.34, 8.35
 experience of: 2.11, 7.2
 graduates: 2.9
 head: 1.6, 1.8, 4.1, 4.6, 7.4, 8.46,
8.52, 8.64
 initial training: 2.10, 8.55, 8.59
 in-service training: 8.55, 8.59, 8.65
 meetings of : 4.11
 men: 2.8, 2.13
 needs of: 8.25, 8.42
 other than class: 3.12, 3.14, 4.2, 5.113
7.34
 probationers: 2.12, 7.2, 8.63
 professional development: **8.55–8.65**
 qualifications of: 2.9
 remedial: 2.25
 responsibilities of: 2.14, 5.49, 8.5, 8.56
 specialist: 5.104, 8.5, 8.35, **8.42–8.44**
 strengths of: 3.17, 5.84, 5.114, 6.3
8.40, 8.44, 8.52
 visiting: 8.54
 women: 2.8, 2.13
teaching
 approach: **3.17–3.24, 7.25–7.37**
 class: **8.40–8.44**
 cooperatives: 3.10, 8.44
 direct: 5.54
 method: **3.17–3.24, 7.25–7.37,
8.60–8.61**
 specialist: 8.35, **8.40–8.65**
 space: 2.1
 television: 5.22, 5.43, 5.54, 5.73, 5.98
5.125, 5.134

tests
 diagnostic: 4.8, 8.59
 mathematics: 1.4, 5.64, 6.28, 6.32, 8.21
 objective: 1.4, 1.8, 6.22
 reading: 1.4, 5.17, 6.23–6.27, 8.18
 school devised: 4.7
 selection of pupils: 6.22
 scores for: 6.25–6.28
 standardised: 4.8, 8.59
thematic approach: 5.115
tools, use of: 5.14
topics: 5.118, 5.123, 5.128, 5.129, 6.19
transfer: 8.31
transition, between classes: **4.7–4.8**, 7.21

V

vandalism: 2.20
vertical grouping: 3.2, 3.5, **7.19**, 7.21
visits
 to other schools: 4.10
 by pupils: 3.16, 5.91, 7.8
visitors, use of: 5.42, 5.91
vocabulary: 5.24

W

weather study: 5.135
West Indian speech patterns: 2.24
withdrawal
 area: 2.1
 of pupils: 3.10, 5.29, 7.4, 8.49
work
 cards: 3.7, 5.52, 5.53, 5.65, 5.126,
5.133, 7.30
 inspection of: 1.7
 levels of difficulty: 6.20, 6.21
 planning of: 5.128
 programme of: 4.1, 4.6, 8.32, 8.46
 quality of: 1.7, 4.6, 5.104, 5.110, 6.1
 range of: 7.33
 standards of: 6.1
working atmosphere: 3.17, 7.28, 8.6
writing: 3.6, 5.14, 5.19, 5.29, **5.31–5.38**
8.20
 copied: 5.33
 descriptive: 6.5, 8.20
 narrative: 6.5, 8.20
 skills: 5.14, 5.19, 5.34, 5.37, 5.38
5.45, 8.20
written work, use of: 5.37, 5.38, 6.5, **7.10**

Printed in England for Her Majesty's Stationery Office by Oyez Press Limited
Dd 596179   K44   9/78